JavaScript Projects

Learn by doing

Rory Hering

About the author

Rory Hering is a front-end engineer with over 17 years of experience bringing designs, concepts and ideas into reality. He's seen the progress and development across the online landscape, not only with the technology – like Flash, JavaScript, HTML, CSS, some PHP, Java and machine learning – but also with the people using and relying on it. He studied at Griffith University to earn a Bachelors of Multimedia degree and later completed a Graduate Certificate in Education (Innovative Learning) with the Queensland University of Technology.

Wearing his engineer's hat Rory has worked with a nationally recognised university and then with a rapidly growing international sports company to make highly accessible interactive content and complex data visualisations. Balancing that with an educator's hat Rory has guided others to create solutions to their own problems and help them to explore different options in their code.

Solving a client's problem must come first, and extensive experience has taught him to look at problems from different angles. That's why he decided to write this book. If it gives an idea to another engineer (or someone who wants to be one) that helps to solve a problem they're having then he'll consider it a success.

Acknowledgments

My deepest gratitude is to my family. They're the reason I'm here today. We've been together for each other, good times and bad. Thank you for everything.

I've also had many teachers over the years, too many to count. If you know me and are reading this then it's likely I've learned something vital just from being near you, and for that, thank you.

There's also my great appreciation to the JavaScript community as a whole, and to other engineers I've known and worked with over the years.

Contents

Introduction

There are number of programming languages that have vanished over time, maybe because of their age, change in trends, capabilities or lack of community support. However, JavaScript has grown more popular despite its age, with additional features added over time as an ever-growing community of people (just like you) discover what it's capable of. With its origins as a basic scripting language it has evolved into the core technology for Node.js servers and is the backbone of all front-end frameworks and libraries.

As a front-end technology JavaScript requires minimal setup: all you need to begin is a browser. Online services like JSFiddle, CodePen, CodeSandbox and JSBin allow you to quickly start coding and see results. If you want you could download an integrated development environment (IDE) like VS Code and use one of its many plugins to run a live server to see your code in action. You can even write JavaScript directly into your browser's console and it will execute it for you.

It's a language where you can start with nothing and build entire applications, or start with a pre built library and build something truly special. And don't let the idea of learning the more advanced stuff hold you back. Once you know the basics, you'll be guided through various projects to help you apply your newfound knowledge to more innovative ideas and concepts.

With all the examples and code you're about to see you might be tempted to say: *this would be better as a website so I could just copy what I need*. But if you have the goal of actually learning[1] JavaScript then it's something you need to write yourself: blindly copying the code won't do you any favours.

For whatever reason you've chosen to learn JavaScript, please know that you're not alone in this journey. It might feel that way sometimes because you're reading from a book, but many other people have walked this path on their way to becoming engineers. Many of them learned from books too.

Everyone has started at the bottom and climbed their way to the top, and you have the chance to follow their path before making your own.

---

[1] https://elearningindustry.com/tell-show-do-apply-the-anatomy-of-good-instruction

Front-end or back-end

JavaScript exists in two different flavours. The first (and the original) is a front-end scripting language. The front-end is your internet browser, such as Google Chrome, Microsoft Edge, Mozilla Firefox and the Apple Safari browser. If something changes on a website, whether it's text, video, an image or some user interface element, chances are there's JavaScript running on the page that's making it happen. Some engineers who have less-than-positive thoughts about JavaScript might dislike it being seen as a 'coding' language, but that's their problem.

The second is on the server, or back-end (called Node.js). Most of the time this serves content to your browser, and that can include front-end JavaScript. This code can't interact with the browser like the front-end version can, but it can interact with databases, other servers, create files and powers many sites on the internet.

While there are some differences between the capabilities of the front and back-end versions of JavaScript they both share the same origin, and for the most part their code is identical. The majority of the code in this book can be used on both browsers and servers, but in the rare cases where they can't you'll be told: usually if there's an interface element like a button then they'll only work on the browser.

If this is your first time using any coding language then it's better to learn it for the browser first. Otherwise you'll need to install the Node.js server that's specific to your device (assuming it's supported).

Useful terms

Programming in general has various slogans, terms and definitions that you'll learn over time, but there are some critical ones that you'll find useful.

Prototyping

Think of prototyping as *proof that it works*. It's probably going to be an ugly mess, but it gives you a foundation to work with. You'd never release it as-is, but a working prototype validates the solution to the problem you're hoping to solve.

Iterate

Not even experienced engineers write code correctly on their first try. Instead, they start with a small piece of code, like a function that does very little, and make sure it works first. Then they begin adding more and testing it as they go, iterating over their code and making it better.

This helps the engineer (you) to identify bugs or problems long before it's complete. Writing dozens of lines of code without testing will only bring you pain and suffering. Start small and make sure each change brings your code closer to the goal.

Refactor

Refactoring your code is like saying 'go back and make it better'. After several iterations you might find that there's a better way of handling the data, so it makes sense to change your code.

Software development life cycle (SDLC)

The software development life cycle is a process used by individual engineers and teams to develop software. Its goal is to reduce risks and costs while also ensuring the client gets what they need. It involves several phases:

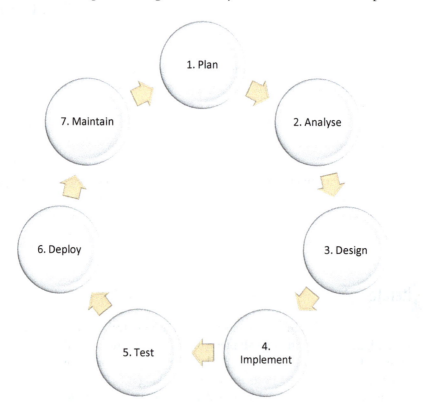

1. **Plan**
   Failing to plan = planning to fail. This is where you ask questions like 'what is the problem?', 'what solutions are already available?' and 'what do we need?'.

2. **Analyse**

   More questions: 'what do we need for solve the problem?', 'can we do this?' and 'who needs to be involved?'. This phase is about determining the requirements and what you're planning to achieve.

3. **Design**

   Now that you know the product's requirements it's time to design. This can involve creating a prototype to prove that a solution is possible, getting insights from your target users, and identify tools and systems to use.

4. **Implement**

   Time to write some code, and don't stop writing until the requirements are met.

5. **Test**

   Let the bug hunt begin: while your code might solve a problem you don't want it to cause new ones. Test that your code not only works on its own but also works with existing code. Test for extreme or strange conditions too as it helps to make it more stable. You're not going to find every bug, but you should have performed enough testing to be confident.

6. **Deploy**

   When your code it ready it's time for deployment. New code and features usually get released on different environments, such as:

   a. Testing – avoids the whole 'it worked on my machine'

   b. Staging – more realistic setup

   c. Canary or Beta (optional) – for users who want to take a chance and be first

   d. Production – everyone gets your code

   This allows new features to be released, debugged and evaluated before the majority of users ever see it. Only your fellow engineers and coworkers will ever see the testing and staging environments and having them help review the product before it goes to production helps increase the confidence.

7. **Maintain**

   You need time to manage bug reports: you tried your best to find every bug, but users will always find more. Different hardware, software, behaviours, experiences, expectations and beliefs will make them use the product in unexpected ways. Your clients might also use the product more than you, so being able to monitor performance helps to plan for the next feature.

Minimum viable product (MVP)

The first product you release should solve the immediate problem and be the most basic solution possible: not a demo or a prototype, but an actual product. A quick solution allows you to ask for feedback without investing a significant amount of time for development. The feedback you get from users allows you to iterate your product until they're happy. Say your users need to get from point A to point B:

The first product you release is a skateboard. It solves the problem and gives you the opportunity to receive feedback from your users. People might not be entirely happy with it, but that's okay — their feedback is more valuable.

The most common piece of feedback you receive is that new users are having some trouble balancing, so you add a new feature: handlebars.

People are beginning to like your product, but ongoing feedback has indicated that as they use it more frequently, users get tired of pushing on the ground with their feet. New features: pedals and a seat.

They love the pedals but as people travel longer distances, they're getting tired. Time to remove the pedals and add an engine.

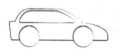

Beginning as a skateboard your product has been through multiple iterations based on the feedback you've received. The latest feedback was about the need to carry more people, and solve an issue about the weather. The result: a car.

Building and releasing the skateboard was quick and effective. If you had decided to create a car from the beginning then chances are you would have spent the same amount of time on the wheels, frame or doors without a single user trying it.

Iterating an MVP also allows you to pivot if (or when) situations change. If the first bit of feedback you receive was 'we need it to cross the river too' then your next release after the skateboard could involve making the board larger, more buoyant and maybe adding a sail.

Commenting

Comments in code (not the comments on a video or post) are a useful way of documenting what you've done so that another engineer can see what you're doing. A language like JavaScript is usually easy to read, but sometimes the overall code can become complex, so adding some comments to help others figure out what you've done is a massive help.

Others doesn't just mean co-workers: it can also be you in several months when you need to make some changes. In JavaScript a comment can be written in two ways:

```
// Single line
```

Use two forward-slashes to write a single line, or:

```
/* Multiple
   lines
*/
```

Use a forward-slash and a star to wrap multiple lines.

Book structure

This book has three main chapters. They are:

1. The basics

Everyone has to start somewhere. If this is your first time working with JavaScript (or you need a refresher) then this is where you should begin. Here you will learn about variables, conditions, loops and functions before moving into promises, sorting and recursion. You'll also get some insider information on some of JavaScript's quirks that might help you avoid problems in the future.

2. Intermediate projects

The training wheels have come off and you're ready to solve some problems. This chapter is to help you apply what you're learned and guide your growth as an engineer by leading you through various projects and scenarios.

3. Advanced projects

Time to explore the big-money topics: games, data analysis, machine learning, drawing, simulations and image manipulation. These are complex projects for any programming language, so take your time and enjoy them.

One more thing:

From this point onward all the code you're about to write is commonly called *vanilla JavaScript*. There are no additional requirements like third-party libraries or dependencies that are needed, no build steps or pipelines, and no specific prior knowledge.

And when you understand what it can do then working with third-party libraries and tools becomes easier. If you want to re-use or republish the code in this book, please know that it's available under the MIT License (just the `code`, not the rest of the book):

Getting started

Before you begin writing JavaScript there are three things you need to have to get the most out of it:

1. the desire to learn,
2. a way to write the code, and
3. a way to run the code

If you're reading this then step 1 is complete! Now for step 2. JavaScript, like the majority of programming languages, uses something called plain-text files: they're a very basic kind of file that you can create and edit in a variety of ways. JavaScript files use the `js` file extension:

- `index.js`
- `app.js`

And if you open them in *any* text editor, on *any* device or operating system they will have the same contents. A word processor *could* be used to create and edit a JavaScript file, but it wouldn't be reliable. Keep it simple and use a text editor, software or service that will keep them as plain-text files.

For step 3: JavaScript, like the majority of programming languages, uses your code (or text instructions) and is interpreted by something called a *parser*. The parser reads the code and outputs the result (if an output is in your code of course). For JavaScript the most common parser is in your internet browser.

If you're using JSFiddle, CodePen, CodeSandbox or JSBin then they'll handle the heavy lifting, but if you want to go *old-school* then you need to create both an HTML file and a JavaScript file.

Quick summary of HTML files (HyperText Markup Language): like JavaScript files they're also plain-text files and they use elements to represent the structure of the page, like this **index.html** file:

```
<!DOCTYPE html>
<html>
<head>
  <title>Basic setup</title>
</head>
<body>
  <script src="./app.js"></script>
</html>
```

The browser reads this file – from top to bottom – and outputs the page. Your JavaScript is run with the script element:

```
<script src="./app.js"></script>
```

The **src** (source) attribute has the file path to your JavaScript file between the quotes. This tells your browser to also open the file as it builds the page.

Browsers only read the JavaScript when they're used in a HTML file, and only some browsers let you run HTML pages without a server. If you create a HTML and an installed browser claims it then chances are it will let you open it:

Mozilla's FireFox browser will let you open the **image-filters.html** file, and that file has a script element that opens **image-filters.js**.

If your browser won't do it and you don't want to use a service then you'll need to go old-school and run a web server. Search for 'HTML server download', read the instructions and find the one that works for you.

The basics

Right now, there are two basic yet very important things you need to know to help in your journey to learn JavaScript, and the first is viewing the console. You will see multiple lines like this:

```
console.log('Hello, World!');
```

While it's usually different for every browser – and even that can change over time – as a first step you should search for 'how to view my browser console'. When you get the console panel open, you're ready to begin. If you're using an online service like JSFiddle then a console pane might already be open.

The other important thing is to enjoy yourself. Running JavaScript on the browser isn't going to corrupt your device or mentally scar you for life. JavaScript code is 'sandboxed' in the browser, which means it can't read, change or delete any file on your devices' storage. It also can't change anything your browser normally does so you're not going to be able to cause any major issues. Many programming languages can do catastrophic things if you're not careful, for example, executing this command in Linux will wipe everything:

```
rm -rf /
```

This chapter is to help you learn the basics. They're the foundations of what you'll need for the rest of the book. Without them you'll quickly find yourself getting lost with some of the more powerful frameworks and tools, and that will only lead to a negative experience.

Like many programming language JavaScript is read left-to-right. This is most likely from code's origins in mathematics. Take the formula to calculate the area of a circle:

$$A = \pi r^2$$

A is the area you want to calculate, π is the value of Pi (3.14… to infinity) and r^2 is the radius of the circle multiplied by itself. A, π and r are called **variables**: they represent the **values** in the formula. The value of π is known, but the area (A) isn't known until the radius (r) is.

This is what the area of a circle formula could look like in JavaScript:

```
const radius = 2;
const area = Math.PI * (radius * radius);
console.log(area); // 12.566370614359172
```

In this example the `radius` of the circle equals 2, which now allows you to calculate the `area`. The single equals character (`=`) tells JavaScript what the `area` variable should be. But this:

```
Math.PI * (radius * radius) = area;
```

This example makes no sense, and your code won't work because it breaks that left-to-right rule. JavaScript has to:

1. allocate space in memory for the variable: `const area`
2. read the expression: `Math.PI * (radius * radius)`
3. calculate the result of the expression: `12.566370614359172`
4. and then set the value of the variable: `=`

Lastly is the semi-colon (`;`). This is a way to tell JavaScript that it's the **end of an expression**. It's not required, and some engineers don't use them at all, but you will see it in all the examples as a visual reminder that what you've written will resolve into a value. It's doesn't represent the end of the line because there are some situations where you wouldn't use it.

Keep these things in mind when writing JavaScript and you should have no problems.

Variables

A variable is a way to represent data and values in your code. It consists of three things:

1. A *name*: a unique and symbolic name that can be used to reference it in your code. There are some rules when making a variable in JavaScript:
    a. No spaces, hyphens, brackets or other special characters. Stick to letters, numbers and if necessary, underscores.
    b. They must start with a letter.
    c. The name is case-sensitive, so `name`, `Name` and `NAME` are three different variables.
    d. Not a reserved word like `if`, `void`, `delete`, `else`, and `return`. There's a full list at the end of this book.
2. The *type*: variables can vary in the data they represent, like Strings, Numbers, Booleans, Arrays, Objects and Functions. In vanilla JavaScript the type is determined by the next part...
3. The *value*: the actual data you want to use.

In JavaScript there's other things to consider: like the declaration:

-   `const`: the value won't change (it's *constant*)
-   `let`: the value will change
-   `var`: the original declaration (not used often anymore)

There's also the scope of the variable. Look at this:

```
const isLiked = true;

if (isLiked) {
  const message = 'You liked this';
}
console.log(message)
```

The boolean variable **isLiked** equals **true**, so the **message** variable is set. Unfortunately, it's set inside a code block (code between curly brackets { }) and can't be used outside of it. If you did want to use the **message** after it has been set you'd need to raise it to a higher level:

```
const isLiked = true;
let message;

if (isLiked) {
  message = 'You liked this';
}
console.log(message)
```

The message is declared and if **isLiked** is **true**, then it's set inside the **if** condition. And if you don't know what a boolean variable is...

Booleans

There are **10** types of people in the world: those who *think* they understand the binary joke, those who don't, and those who recognise **0**, **1** and **2** as real values (binary **00** = **0**, binary **01** = **1** and binary **10** = **2**).

For Boolean variables you only need to use the first two: **0** and **1**, or **false** and **true**. This type of variable is a great when it comes to making decisions about what happens next in your code.

```
const isLiked = true;
if (isLiked) {
  // ...
}
```

In the above example the `isLiked` variable will determine if the code in the `if` condition will be executed. Because the value is `true` the code (not shown) will be run, but if it was `false`:

```
const isLiked = false;
if (isLiked) {
  // ...
}
```

Then the condition will skip over the code and continue to the next. In regular JavaScript it's rare for a `const` boolean variable to be set like `const isLiked = false` because if you know a value will be `true` or `false` at all times then there's no reason for it to exist. A better way to set a boolean variable is like this:

```
const isAfternoon = new Date().getHours() >= 12;
let message = 'Good morning!';

if (isAfternoon) {
  message = 'Good afternoon!';
}
console.log(message);
```

In this example the `isAfternoon` value is dependent on a `Date` object (more on them soon). If the current number of hours is greater than or equal to 12 then the `message` is changed. And as you can see, the `message` is a string, so...

Strings

```
const message = 'Hello, world!';
```

Any value surrounded by quotes is considered a string. And you have some options too – those were single quotes, here's double quotes:

```
const message = "Hello, world!";
```

And these are backtick quotes:

```
const message = `Hello, world!`;
```

The backticks allow for something called template literals, which gives you more options in what can go into those strings. For example, if you wanted to put your name into the message (without having to hard-code it):

```
const name = prompt('What is your name?');
const message = `Hello, ${name}!`;
console.log(message);
```

JavaScript will **prompt** for your name and then inject it into the **message** value when it's declared.

Strings also have some methods that can help you. The **trim** method removes spaces that are before and after any other characters:

```
const message = '   Good morning!     ';
console.log(message.trim());
```

The **replace** method allows you to change one part of the string for another:

```
const message = 'Good morning!';
console.log(message.replace('morning', 'afternoon'));
```

There are several others, but one of the most useful methods is **split**. This method takes the string (called a delimiter) and literally splits it into an array of strings, for example, splitting a tongue twister:

```
const toungueTwister = 'peter piper picked a pack of pickled
peppers';
console.log(toungueTwister.split('p'));
```

And the result:

```
["", "eter ", "i", "er ", "icked a ", "ack of ", "ickle", "ed ",
"e", "ers"]
```

If no string – or an empty string – is used to split the string, like this:

```
console.log(toungueTwister.split(''));
```

Then you'll get an array of individual characters:

```
["p", "e", "t", "e", "r", " ", "p", "i", "p", "e", "r", " ", "p",
"i", "c", "k", "e", "d", " ", "a", " ", "p", "a", "c", "k", " ",
"o", "f", " ", "p", "i", "c", "k", "l", "e", "d", " ", "p", "e",
"p", "p", "e", "r", "s"]
```

Speaking of arrays…

Arrays

Think of arrays as a list of values. Let's say you wanted an array of fruit:

```
const fruit = ['apple', 'orange', 'banana'];
```

Arrays use square brackets [ ] to contain their items, so the **fruit** array has three items. If you wanted to add another, you can use the **push** method:

```
fruit.push('blueberry');
```

The blueberry string has now been pushed into the end of the array. You can get each value inside an array by giving it an index between the square brackets:

```
console.log(fruit[0]);
```

Remember that boolean/binary joke from earlier? This is why zero is so important in languages like JavaScript. Array indexes start at 0, also known as index-0. You can set the index/value relationship yourself, like this:

```
const fruit = [];
fruit[0] = 'apple';
fruit[1] = 'orange';
fruit[2] = 'banana';
```

```
console.log(fruit);

['apple', 'orange', 'banana']
```

But it's not recommended. Say you disagreed with index-0 and wanted to start at 1 for arrays:

```
const fruit = [];
fruit[1] = 'apple';
fruit[2] = 'orange';
fruit[3] = 'banana';
console.log(fruit);
```

You'll get this:

```
[undefined, 'apple', 'orange', 'banana']
```

That **undefined** is another legitimate value, and as a result the **fruit** array now has four values. Here's how you can see how many values are in an array:

```
console.log(fruit.length);
```

Index-0 may seem confusing if you're not used to it, but it should not put you off using arrays as they're very powerful. Remember that string splitting from before? Let's add a bit more to it:

```
const fruit = 'apple, orange, banana, blueberry';
console.log(fruit.split(', '));
```

The **split** method has returned an array of fruits. The original **fruit** string has not changed, see:

```
console.log(fruit.split(', '));
['apple', 'orange', 'banana', 'blueberry']

console.log(fruit);
'apple, orange, banana, blueberry'
```

You pushed 'blueberry' into the array earlier, so what if you wanted to remove it?

```
const fruit = ['apple', 'orange', 'banana', 'blueberry'];
console.log(fruit.pop());
```

The output is 'blueberry'. The **pop** method removes the last value from the array and returns it.

The **shift** does the same thing except it's for the first item – removes it from the beginning of the array and returns it:

```
const fruit = ['apple', 'orange', 'banana', 'blueberry'];
console.log(fruit.shift());
```

But what if you wanted to use the items as values for other variables? You could reference them by their indexes:

```
const fruit = ['apple', 'orange', 'banana', 'blueberry'];
const firstFruit = fruit[0];
const secondFruit = fruit[1];
const thirdFruit = fruit[2];
```

Or you use something called destructuring (not a typo). This gives you the ability to 'unpack' values into their own variables and use them in other ways:

```
const fruit = ['apple', 'orange', 'banana', 'blueberry'];
const [first, second, ...others] = fruit;
console.log(first); // apple
console.log(second); // orange
console.log(others); // ['banana', 'blueberry']
```

It starts with the same array of fruits but instead of using the index of each item to get the values as before, you declare a new variable by assigning it to the necessary index on the left-hand-side of the equals (=) character. Because of the ... used before the **others** variable JavaScript has spread the remaining values into another array.

If you just wanted the first value, you could use this:

```
const fruit = ['apple', 'orange', 'banana', 'blueberry'];
```

```
const [first] = fruit;
console.log(first); // apple
```

Or for a more useful example:

```
const date = '2021-10-20';
const [year, month, day] = date.split('-');
```

The **date** string has been split by the hyphen, and through destructuring you can get the **year**, **month** and **day** values as their own variables. Also, the **date** string has not been changed so you can use it for other things later on.

Arrays have a lot of methods you'll find useful but there are some you might find very handy: **sort**, **forEach**, **map**, **filter**, and **reduce**. Sorting has been given its own section, so this will focus on the others. Each of these use a callback function to determine what happens in each of them.

```
array.forEach(callbackFunction);
const result = array.map(callbackFunction);
const result = array.filter(callbackFunction);
const result = array.reduce(
  callbackFunction, initialValue
);
```

Note that **map**, **filter**, and **reduce** will return a new array. The contents of the new array will depend on what's in the callback function.

The **forEach** method loops through all the items in an array so you can do something *with* them (not *to* them). This example outputs each fruit as uppercase characters:

```
const fruits = ['apple', 'banana', 'orange'];
fruits.forEach((fruit) => {
  console.log(fruit.toUpperCase());
});
// APPLE
// BANANA
// ORANGE
```

That **fruit** variable is an argument of the callback function and is the current item that the **forEach** method is looking at. So, the code between the curly brackets ({}) will run three times as that's how many items are in the array. More items: the more times the code will run.

The **map** method loops through all the items in an array and creates a new array of items. This doesn't change the original array, but it lets you create a new one with different values. In this example it creates a new array with some additional information about each fruit:

```
const fruits = ['apple', 'banana', 'orange'];
const report = fruits.map((fruit) => {
  return `${fruit} is a fruit with ${fruit.length} characters`;
});
console.log(report);
// [
//   'apple is a fruit with 5 characters',
//   'banana is a fruit with 6 characters',
//   'orange is a fruit with 6 characters'
// ]
```

The **filter** method loops through all the items in an array and creates a new array of items that match your requirements (and again the original is unchanged). The callback function used in the **filter** must return either **true** to include the value, or **false** to include it. This example creates an array of fruits that has six characters:

```
const fruits = ['apple', 'banana', 'orange'];
const longFruit = fruits.filter((fruit) => {
  return fruit.length === 6;
});
console.log(longFruit); // ['banana', 'orange']
```

You can see the difference between **map** and **filter**: **map** returns the value that will be used in the new array and **filter** determines if the value should be in it.

Last but not least there's **reduce**. This is a very powerful method that can create entirely new structures from an array. For this example it will loop through the original array and create an object (more on those soon) that uses the fruit name as a key and the number of characters as the value:

```
const fruits = ['apple', 'banana', 'orange'];
const report = fruits.reduce((accumulator, fruit) => {
  accumulator[fruit] = fruit.length;
  return accumulator;
}, {});
console.log(report);
```

The result is this:

```
{
  apple: 5,
  banana: 6,
  orange: 6
}
```

Last but not least is the spread operator. Using three periods/full-stops before a declared array extracts the values. Say you wanted to copy an array:

```
const numbers = [1, 2, 3, 4, 5];
console.log([...numbers]); // [1, 2, 3, 4, 5]
```

On its own it's not very exciting, but you can use this to combine arrays:

```
const numbers = [10, 9, 8, 7, 6];
console.log([...numbers, 5, 4, 3, 2, 1]);
// [10, 9, 8, 7, 6, 5, 4, 3, 2, 1]
```

Moving onto numbers...

Numbers

When declaring string values you need to surround them with quotes or JavaScript may treat them as other variables. When it comes to numbers no quotes are needed:

```
const number = 64;
```

And for decimals:

```
const floatingNumber = 63.99999;
```

But so much more can be done! What if you had a number that was declared as a string, or in this example inside a string and you just wanted the value? `parseInt` function to the rescue:

```
const numberInString = '64px';
const number = parseInt(numberAsString);
```

The **parseInt** function will extract the first number value it can find. It does mean that you'll only get the first 1 in this example:

```
const equation = '1 + 2 + 3 + 4';
console.log(parseInt(equation));
```

There's a similar one for numbers with decimal places: **parseFloat**:

```
const pi = '3.14159';
console.log(parseFloat(pi));
```

Keep in mind that both of these functions stop when they don't find a number value. That's why the **parseInt** function stopped at 1, and why the next example will return **NaN**, or Not a Number:

```
const sentence = 'The value of pi is 3.14159.';
console.log(parseFloat(sentence));
```

The first character in the string is 'T' so the function ends immediately, and 'T' is not a number so that's the result you get.

If you *really* wanted to extract the number in the **sentence** variable there is a way. Whole books have been written about this part, but you can get a taste here.

Regular Expressions are a way to match patterns in strings, and one of the infinite ways they can be used is to extract the numeric characters from a string so they can be converted into a number.

```
const sentence = 'The value of pi is 3.14159.';
const number = parseFloat(
  sentence.match(/\d+\.?\d*/g)[0]
```

```
);
console.log(number); // 3.14159
```

Let's break down that regular expression used in the **match** method:

- The first and last forward slash **/** tells JavaScript that it's the start and end of a regular expression
- **\d** matches any digit
- **+** says to match the previous token (\d) once to as many times as possible
- **\.** is an escaped period or full-stop (without the backslash escape the period/full-stop will have a different meaning)
- **?** says to match the previous token zero or once
- **\d** as above
- ***** says to match the previous token zero to as many times as possible
- the **g** at the end is the 'global' option so it won't stop at one match

So that's 'match any digit once to infinite times until there is an optional full stop, and keep matching if there are more digits'. Again, there are whole books written about regular expressions if you want to go down that path.

Despite their complexity they are very powerful. That returned match is an array of string values, and the first one is the value you want to convert into a decimal number. You can take this even further to get all the numbers from a string:

```
const sentence = 'I have 3 apples and you have 6 oranges';
const numbers = sentence.match(/\d+\.?\d*/g)
                        .map((number) => parseInt(number));
console.log(numbers); // [3, 6]
```

That will extract the 3 and the 6 from the sentence: the regex (short for regular expression) matches the two numeric strings and returns them as an array. The **map** method then converts them into numbers.

Let's go back to the basics. Numbers and math go together, and it just so happens JavaScript has a whole bunch of **Math** you can use. You can generate a random number with the **random** method:

```
const number = Math.random();
console.log(number); // 0.????
```

The result is a decimal number between 0 and 1. And if you wanted a whole random number between 0 and 100:

```
const number = Math.floor(Math.random() * 101);
```

The **floor** method will round down the value it's given. In this case the random value, after its been multiplied by 101, will be rounded down to the nearest whole value. If a method called **floor** exists to round numbers down, what would you call a method to round them up?

```
const number = 3.141592653589793;
const numberRoundedDown = Math.floor(number); // 3
const numberRoundedUp = Math.ceil(number); // 4
const numberRounded = Math.round(number); // 3
```

Yep, **ceil** (short for ceiling) rounds numbers up to the nearest whole value. The third part is **round** which will round the value to the nearest whole number, so it will go up or down depending on if the decimal is:

- greater than (or equal to) **.5** – round up
- less than **.5** – round down

You can use **Math.sin**, **Math.cos** and **Math.tan** for trigonometry (there's *a lot* more methods for trigonometry too), **Math.sqrt** to find the square root of a number, and then there's the method to give you the minimum and maximum values: **min** and **max**:

```
const minValue = Math.min(10, 9, 8, 5, 4, 3, 2, 1);
const maxValue = Math.max(10, 9, 8, 5, 4, 3, 2, 1);
console.log(minValue); // 1
console.log(maxValue); // 10
```

The **min** and **max** methods accept multiple arguments and return the value that meets the method's criteria. As a rule, you don't want to repeat values like that (DRY: Don't Repeat Yourself). You can declare those values in an array and use the spread operator (**...**) to get the **min** and **max**:

```
const numbers = [10, 9, 8, 7, 6, 5, 4, 3, 2, 1];
const minValue = Math.min(...numbers);
const maxValue = Math.max(...numbers);
```

```
console.log(minValue); // 1
console.log(maxValue); // 10
```

Objects

Objects are values made of other values:

```
const user = {
  name: 'Alex',
  age: 30,
  email: 'alex@example.com',
  orders: [
    { id: 1, name: 'iPhone', price: 1599 },
    { id: 2, name: 'MacBook Pro', price: 3299 },
    { id: 3, name: 'iMac', price: 1799 }
  ]
};
```

Specifically, objects are a list of key/value pairs. For the above `user` variable, `name`, `age`, `email` and `orders` are the keys with everything afterwards being the values. And those values can be different types too: you might have noticed that `orders` is an array of objects.

While arrays use an index to get and set their items, objects use their keys to do the same. To get the price of Alex's first order you can do this:

```
console.log(user.orders[0].price); // 1599
```

The `[0]` on the orders array might be familiar but the dot notation for objects is new. If you just wanted the user's name, you start with the variable name and reference the key you want with a full-stop in between:

```
console.log(user.name); // Alex
```

You could also use the key as a string index similar to arrays:

```
console.log(user['name']); // Alex
```

If it's just a one-word key then you'd probably stick to the dot notation, unless you have a key that's more complex:

```
const user = {
  // ...
  'first-name': 'Alex',
  'last-name': 'Smith',
};
console.log(user['first-name']); // Alex
```

You can't use `user.first-name` because JavaScript will think the hyphen in `first-name` is for subtraction. In that example it's better to use the string index.

Objects also have their own methods: let's look at **keys** and **values**!

```
console.log(Object.keys(user));
// ['name', 'age', 'email', 'orders']
```

`Object.keys` extracts the keys from the object and returns them as an array. But only the highest-level ones – you won't see those nested in the `orders` array. Do you want to take a guess what `Object.values` does?

```
console.log(Object.values(user));
// ['Alex', 30, 'alex@example.com', [
//     { id: 1, name: 'iPhone', price: 1599 },
//     { id: 2, name: 'MacBook Pro', price: 3299 },
//     { id: 3, name: 'iMac', price: 1799 },
//   ]
// ]
```

You can also use destructuring too. Like arrays you supply it with the keys you want to extract (but using the curly brackets instead of the square ones):

```
const { name, email, ...rest } = user;
console.log(name); // 'Alex'
console.log(email); // 'alex@example.com'
console.log(rest); // { age: 30, orders: [...] }
```

Any and all keys supplied like that will return those values as new variables. If you don't provide the key, then it won't be declared as a variable.

You might have noticed the return of the spread operator. Just like arrays it extracts the values, except in this example a new **rest** variable (or any other name you want) will be created with the **age** and **orders** as properties.

Let's say you wanted the name and email of the user so you could send them a list of their previous orders:

```
const { name, email, ...rest } = user;
const contact = { name, email };
const orders = rest.orders.map((order) => order.name);
console.log(contact);
// { name: 'Alex', email: 'alex@example' }
console.log(orders);
// ['iPhone', 'MacBook Pro', 'iMac']
```

The **name** and **email** have been destructured, the new **contact** variable has been made, and the new **orders** array was made by mapping the name from the original **orders**.

Whenever you're creating objects a key and value is necessary. The **contact** variable *appears* to have been created without a value, but you can thank JavaScript for a little shortcut. Once upon a time this would have been necessary:

```
const contact = {
  name: name,
  email: email
};
```

But now JavaScript lets you just provide the key and as long as the key is a variable then it creates the key/value paring for you. This allows for some very powerful code to be written. With the same original data you could create a report of the user to be used for marketing:

```
const user = {
  name: 'Alex',
  age: 30,
  email: 'alex@example.com',
  orders: [
    { id: 1, name: 'iPhone', price: 1599 },
    { id: 2, name: 'MacBook Pro', price: 3299 },
```

```
    { id: 3, name: 'iMac', price: 1799 },
  ]
};


const { name, email, ...rest } = user;
const contact = { name, email };
const marketing = {
  trackingId: '0c8e8b5a-8a1a-4d1d-8c0a-6fcdcf7d4d05',
  ...contact,
  totalSpent: rest.orders.reduce(
    (total, order) => total + order.price,
    0
  )
};
```

The **totalSpent** could have been calculated before the **marketing** object was declared, but it's good to see different ways to work. The result is:

```
console.log(marketing);
// {
//   trackingId: '0c8e8b5a-8a1a-4d1d-8c0a-6fcdcf7d4d05',
//   name: 'Alex',
//   email: 'alex@example.com',
//   totalSpent: 6687
// }
```

And now, what if you wanted to remove a key and value? Yes, you could create a new variable with only the ones you want to keep, but JavaScript lets you do something else:

```
delete user.orders;
console.log(user);
// { name: 'Alex', age: 30, email: 'alex@example.com' }
```

You can only use **delete** on an object's keys. This does modify the object, but if you're only removing one or two values it should be okay.

Dates

When it comes to dates there's something very important for you to understand: it's a Unix *timestamp*. Once it's declared, and no matter how you declare it, it remains as a timestamp. And these timestamps equal the number of milliseconds between January 1st, 1970 (Co-ordinated Universal Time, or UTC) and the date you declare. So if you declare a **Date** like this:

```
const today = new Date();
```

The **today** variable – behind the scenes – sets the timestamp to today's date and time using the UTC time zone, *not your time zone*. When you get or set parts of a date variable it handles the conversion between the UTC timestamp and what you want. To see the timestamp you can use this:

```
console.log(today.getTime());
```

Dates are complicated in JavaScript. You can set them like this using strings (both with and without a time):

```
const now = new Date('2024-01-01');
const nowWithTime = new Date('2024-01-01T00:00:00');
```

Note the format of **YYYY-MM-DD**, and the much longer **YYYY-MM-DDTHH:mm:ss.sssZ**.
The four-digit year is the minimum needed if you don't want to declare today's date. If you prefer to declare them as numbers, you can do the same like this:

```
const now = new Date(2024, 0, 1);
const nowWithTime = new Date(2024, 0, 1, 0, 0, 0);
```

That **0** used for the month is not a typo – when represented as numbers the months start from **0**. Like other languages JavaScript inherited that process from another language called C, and that has the same index-0 for months.

```
const now = new Date('2024-01-01');
console.log(now.toDateString());
```

```
const alsoNow = new Date(2024, 0, 1);
console.log(alsoNow.toDateString());
```

Yep, give it a try: they're the same. Remember, dates are complicated. If you have to work with dates more frequently then it's *strongly recommended* you spend some time reviewing a date library to handle this for you. Others have generously donated their time to create these tools to use so you don't have to struggle with them.

Conditional statements

The previous section gave some examples of conditionals, but here we'll go a little deeper. These conditional statements help control the flow of your code and allow it to react to inputs differently, depending on what you want it to do.

If...else

The most well-known one is the **if** statement:

```
if (true) {
  console.log('Hello, World!');
}
```

The only thing the **if** statement cares about is if the resolved value that's between the two parentheses **()** is **true**. In the above example it's *clearly* **true** so the words **Hello, World!** are printed out.

There are times you want different things to happen depending on other conditions. Let's say you need to show a message depending on the time of the day – 'good morning' if it's before noon, 'good afternoon' if it's before 6pm, and 'good evening' if it's after that.

```
const time = new Date().getHours();
if (time < 12) {
```

```
  console.log('Good morning!');
} else if (time < 18) {
  console.log('Good afternoon!');
} else {
  console.log('Good evening!');
}
```

Or reversed like this:

```
if (time > 18) {
  console.log('Good evening!');
} else if (time > 12) {
  console.log('Good afternoon!');
} else {
  console.log('Good morning!');
}
```

But *not* like this:

```
if (time < 18) {
  console.log('Good afternoon!');
} else if (time < 12) {
  console.log('Good morning!');
} else {
  console.log('Good evening!');
}
```

Why? Conditional statements 'catch' the operation when their conditions are met. The first two examples work because they operate at the extremes:

- 0 to 12, 12 to 18, everything else (low to high)
- 23 to 18, 18 to 12, everything else (high to low)

In the third example you will never see 'Good morning!' because the `time < 18` will also catch the `time < 12`. Any time that's less than 18 hours will always resolve to `true` in the first condition, so it will never reach the next one. Sure, it will output 'Good evening!' when the hours are more than 18, but that middle `else if` will never be reached.

These statements are great when working with single or multiple conditions and variables. Using logic operators like **&&** (and), **||** (or) and **!** (logical not) can make them very elaborate too. If you wanted different messages depending on time, mood and if it was a weekend, you could write something like this:

```
const time = new Date().getHours();
const mood = 'angry';
if (time < 12 && mood === 'happy' && !isWeekend) {
  // ...
} else {
  // ...
}
```

This example gives you some very granular controls over what code is executed: if the time is before noon, the mood is happy and it's not the weekend then you can show a different message compared to the when the time or mood is different.

Switch

While `if` statements allow for more control, `switch` statements (or blocks) are more specific. Switch statements only check the value of the resolved variable. Let's say you wanted to show a message based on your mood:

```
const mood = 'happy';
switch (mood) {
  case 'happy':
    console.log('I am happy!');
    break;
  case 'sad':
    console.log('I am sad!');
    break;
  default:
    console.log('I am neither happy nor sad!');
}
```

That `switch(...)` determines the result depending on what is resolved between those parentheses:

- mood === happy: I am happy!
- mood === sad: I am sad!
- else (default): I am neither happy nor sad!

If you wanted to work with a range (like the time examples) you *could* do something like this:

```
const time = new Date().getHours();
switch (time) {
  case 0:
  case 1:
  case 2:
  case 3:
  case 4:
  case 5:
  case 6:
  case 7:
  case 8:
  case 9:
  case 10:
  case 11:
    console.log('Good morning!');
    break;
  case 12:
  // case 13 - case 17
    console.log('Good afternoon!');
    break;
  default:
    console.log('Good evening!');
}
```

And the person reviewing your code would give you a funny look and wonder if you really know what you're talking about. Switch statements are best when working with discrete values. If you have to work with a range that requires multiple options, stick with the `if` statements.

Remember that **switch** statements are driven by their resolved value:

```
switch (mood === 'happy') {
  case true:
    console.log('I am happy!');
    break;
  case false:
    console.log('I am sad!');
    break;
}
```

Again, that could have been another **if** statement but it's good to have options. Here is where **switch** really shines though: that time example, despite being a bad one, did show **switch**'s ability to catch the unknowns that might not have been caught by an **if** statement. If you were to miss that final **else** in your code, JavaScript wouldn't care. Admittedly it wouldn't care if you missed that **default** at the end of the **switch**, but if you're working on a larger project that has linting tools then it's likely to give you a warning.

And then there's the performance: **switch** isn't checking the conditions every time as it's already resolved the value. The hard work is done; it just has to determine what to do next.

Ternary

Sometimes you just want something simple. When that time comes then a ternary condition is what you need. Take this regular if/else statement that sets a value:

```
let message;
if (mood === 'happy') {
  message = 'I am happy!';
} else {
  message = 'I am sad!';
}
console.log(message); // I am happy!
```

If that's all you need to do, then you can simplify your code to make it much easier to read. Try it like this:

```
const message = mood === 'happy'
  ? 'I am happy!'
  : 'I am sad!';

console.log(message); // I am happy!
```

Technically it's a one-liner. The **mood === 'happy'** condition is still there, but the **?** and **:** are what is returned if the result is **true** or **false** respectively. The structure of a ternary statement is like this:

```
const message = (true) ? 'value if true' : 'value if false';
```

Just like the **if** statements it only cases about the resolved value between the parentheses (though they're often omitted). The code after the **?** is for when it resolves as true, and the code after the **:** is for when it's not.

You can nest these, but unless formatting is maintained they can begin to become unruly:

```
const message = mood === 'happy'
  ? 'I am happy!'
  : mood === 'sad'
    ? 'I am sad!'
    : 'I am neither happy nor sad!';
```

Try...catch

Errors happen. If your code is relying on data that you can't trust, like from a database, form or file, chances are you're going to encounter an error. Whether it's because your code wasn't ready for some value, server timeout or a bad connection, it's necessary for your code to accept that an error can happen. You also need it to be able to recover.

That's where **try/catch** comes in. Unlike the other conditionals it's not about specific variables, ranges or discrete values. Think of it like this: **try** the code, and *if* it doesn't work, **catch** the error before the user does.

Let's say you have a function that gets the user's name, and you want to output that name in a message:

```
const name = fetchName();
if (name) {
  console.log(`Hello, ${name}!`);
} else {
  console.log('Hi, something went wrong!');
}
```

This code is fine, there's nothing wrong with it. What about now:

```
const name = fetchName().trim();
if (name) {
  console.log(`Hello, ${name}!`);
} else {
  console.log('Hi, something went wrong!');
}
```

That **trim()** removes any spaces before and after the **name** – assuming a string value is returned. If that **fetchName** function doesn't return a string value then JavaScript will throw an error and those messages won't be seen.
Try this:

```
try {
  const name = fetchName().trim();
  console.log(`Hello, ${name}!`);
} catch (error) {
  console.log('Hi, something went wrong!');
}
```

Now if *anything* goes wrong in that **try** block, the **catch** block will take care of it. That **error** argument will have information about that happened and where, so when you're testing make sure you can see what that information is just in case it's something you should fix.

```
try {
  const name = fetchName().trim();
  console.log(`Hello, ${name}!`);
```

```
} catch (error) {
  if (error instanceof TypeError) {
    // ...
  } else if (error instanceof ReferenceError) {
    // ...
  } else if (error instanceof RangeError) {
    // ...
  } else {
    // ...
  }
  console.log('Hi, something went wrong!');
}
```

The **instanceof** is a check for the type: just like variables have types, errors have them too.

There's an optional part to the **try/catch**: **finally**.

```
try {
  const name = fetchName().trim();
  console.log(`Hello, ${name}!`);
} catch (error) {
  console.log('Hi, something went wrong!');
} finally {
  console.log('Bye!');
}
```

Regardless of what happens, the **finally** block will always execute. This is an opportunity to clean up the data or show some kind of feedback. If you don't need to use it, then don't include it.

Loops

Loops were briefly looked at with some of the array methods, like **forEach**. Except loops aren't reserved just for arrays. You can use loops for other things, like with numbers, or searching for something specific in a pile of data. There are several versions, but the big two are here.

for

A basic **for** loop looks like this:

```
for (let i = 0; i < 10; i++) {
  console.log(i);
}
```

The loop has four parts:

1. the initialisation: **let i = 0**
   - executed once before the rest of the code block
2. the condition: **i < 10**
   - when this is no longer **true**, the loop stops
3. the afterthought: **i++**
   - executed every time the iteration finishes
4. the code to be executed: **console.log(i);**

As long as the condition is **true**, the loop will continue to run iterations of the code, in this case, the **console.log(i);**. After each iteration the **i** variable increases by 1.

while

This loop is a little different:

```
let i = 0;
while (i < 10) {
  console.log(i);
  i++;
}
```

The condition is still there (**i < 10**), but the initialisation is before the loop and the afterthought is literally at the end. By the way, if you want a bad-time with loops forget to update the counter or have a condition that will always be **true**:

```
let i = 0;
while (i < 10) {
  console.log(i);
}
```

```
while (true) {
  console.log('Welcome to an infinite loop!');
}
```

Stopping

These loops are capable of doing something **sort**, **forEach**, **map**, **filter**, and **reduce** can't do, and that's stop. If you have an array of 10,000 values and you need to process the data but stop if one of them matches a specific condition, like searching for a needle in a haystack:

```
const needle = { id: 1 };
const haystack = [{ id: 2 }, needle, { id: 0 }];
```

You've added the needle to the haystack. Using the **forEach** method seems like a good idea to find it again, until you realise it won't stop:

```javascript
haystack.forEach((item) => {
  if (item === needle) {
    console.log('needle');
    break;
  }
  console.log(item);
});
```

That **break** can't be used. Even though you found the needle the loop will continue until it processes everything. But a regular **for** loop doesn't have the same issue. This example shows what you want:

```javascript
for (let i = 0; i < 10; i++) {
  if (i === 5) {
    break;
  }
  console.log(i);
}
```

If the condition **i === 5** is **true** then the loop should stop. Until then the data can continue to be processed. So now you can apply it to your massive array:

```javascript
for (let i = 0, imax = haystack.length; i < imax; i++) {
  const item = haystack[i];
  if (item === needle) {
    console.log('needle');
    break;
  }
  console.log(haystack[i]);
}
```

When the needle is found, it will stop the loop. This needle-in-a-haystack example is a great way to show how one kind of loop is superior to others, providing that a *specific* use-case it met (i.e. stopping when found). In most cases the array methods are fine, and in some ways have been optimised by various JavaScript engines to perform better than their more manual counterparts.

It's important to understand what the use-case is for your situation and determine the best course of action.

Functions

Functions are wrappers around your code that you can call when required. Let's say you have this line:

```
console.log('Hello, world!');
```

You can wrap that in a function, like this:

```
const init = () => {
  console.log('Hello, world!');
};
```

You can declare them the same way as other variables. The above example uses the modern arrow function to declare it, but you can still use the original:

```
function init() {
  console.log('Hello, world!');
}
```

To actually make it execute the code you need to *call* the function:

```
init();
```

The open and close parenthesis ( ) are what makes it different to a variable and are needed to execute the code. But they're not just there for decoration: you can put **arguments** inside. Arguments are a way of passing data to the code inside the function. Let's say you need to calculate the percentage of votes:

```
const percent = (votes / totalVotes) * 100;
```

This is fine until you need to do the same for multiple political parties:

```
const blueberryPercentage = (bbVotes / totalVotes) * 100;
const redberryPercentage = (rbVotes / totalVotes) * 100;
const crushedberryPercentage = (cbVotes / totalVotes) * 100;
```

That's a lot of repetition. When you start repeating code it's time to create a function (aka refactor):

```
const calculatePercentage = (votes, totalVotes) => {
  return (votes / totalVotes) * 100;
};
```

See the **votes** and **totalVotes**? They're arguments: they're like local variables but they can only be used inside the function. Functions also allow you to **return** values that can be used for a variable:

```
const blueberryPercentage =
  calculatePercentage(bbVotes, totalVotes);
const redberryPercentage =
  calculatePercentage(rbVotes, totalVotes);
const crushedberryPercentage =
  calculatePercentage(cbVotes, totalVotes);
```

Even though the first argument, **bbVotes**, **rbVotes** and **cbVotes** are different, the **calculatePercentage** function happily uses the local **votes** argument in the executed code.

When the **calculatePercentage** function is complete it returns the value to the variable. So now if you need to change how the calculation is made and what value is returned you only have to do it on one location.

Function verses method

Functions and methods do the same things. The difference is *what they do it to*. Take an array's `forEach` method: unlike a function you didn't specify the array as one of the arguments. Same for a string's `trim()` method or a number's `toFixed()` method: they act directly on the variable.

Depending on the variable's type you can also do some chaining with the methods:

```
const number = 42;
const firstCharacter = number.toFixed(2).charAt(0);
```

The `toFixed` method returns the number as a string (with two decimal places), which then gives you the ability to use the `charAt` method to return the first character. You could to the same thing with a function:

```
const firstCharacter = (number) => {
  const numberAsString = number.toFixed(2);
  const firstCharacter = numberAsString.charAt(0);
  return firstCharacter;
}
console.log(firstCharacter(42));
```

Depending on your use-case this could be easier or harder for you to read, so it's ultimately up to you how you combine (or don't combine) functions and methods. There are also ways to create new methods for existing types like numbers and strings:

```
Number.prototype.firstCharacter = function() {
  return this.toFixed(2).charAt(0);
};
console.log((42).firstCharacter());
```

But this is often frowned upon. It's called prototype pollution and is considered a vulnerability in JavaScript: not only can you add new methods but also change existing ones.

```
Number.prototype.toFixed = function() {
  return 'Hello, world!';
```

```
};
console.log((42).toFixed(2));
```

Various code repositories and services scan the code stored and look for vulnerabilities like prototype pollution, so as a general rule don't create or update these. Some of the exercises in the later chapters use JavaScript Classes where you can define your own methods and won't throw any warnings or security issues at you.

Methods can also be very strict when it comes to the arguments they accept. With the number's **toFixed** method:

```
const number = 42;
console.log(number.toFixed('hi')); // 42
console.log(number.toFixed(1)); // 42.0
console.log(number.toFixed(0)); // 42
console.log(number.toFixed(-1)); // error
```

A string used as the argument will be the same as a 0, but **toFixed** won't allow a negative value as an argument and throw an error. On the plus side it will tell you why:

```
RangeError: toFixed() digits argument must be between 0 and 100
```

Variables, loops and functions: the spreadsheet version

If JavaScript is your first programming language then understanding things like variables, their types (strings, numbers, arrays, etc...), loops and functions can be daunting even with examples. Chances are you've used some kind of spreadsheet in your life, so it might be good to use that as a foundation and go from there.

Take a look at the following 'spreadsheet':

	A	B
1	Hello	World

The cell **A1** has a value of 'Hello'. Think of **A1** as the variable's name with 'Hello' as its value (and the type is a string). Same with **B1** and its value of 'World'. In JavaScript those variables and values would look like this:

```
const A1 = 'Hello';
const B2 = 'World';
```

The string values of 'Hello' and 'World' are assigned to the **A1** and **B1** variables respectively. It's the same with numbers (except without the quotes):

	A	B
1	10	20

```
const A1 = 10;
const B2 = 20;
```

Great! Now what if you wanted to add the values of **A1** and **B1**? Your spreadsheet might look like this:

	A	B	C
1	10	20	= A1 + B1

The cell **C1** now has an expression/formula in it. The value of **A1** (10) will be added to the value of **B1** (20) and return a value for **C1** (30):

```
const A1 = 10;
const B2 = 20;
const C1 = A1 + B2;
```

Adding two numbers is easy, but what if you had more numbers, like this:

	A	B	C	D	E
1	10	20	30	40	50

Now you could write out variables for each of them:

```
const A1 = 10;
const B1 = 20;
const C1 = 30;
const D1 = 40;
const E1 = 50;
```

But you're not going to add them together like this:

	A	B	C	D	E	F
1	10	20	30	40	50	= A1 + B1 + C1 + D1 + E1

```
const sum = A1 + B1 + C1 + D1 + E1;
```

Instead, you'd make the most of what the spreadsheet gives you:

	A	B	C	D	E	F
1	10	20	30	40	50	= SUM(A1:E1)

It's the same when writing code – work smarter, not harder – and make the most of the tools (in this case: methods) available to you in JavaScript:

```
const A1_E1 = [10, 20, 30, 40, 50]; // row values
const F1 = A1_E1.reduce(
  (acc, value) => acc + value,
  0
); // sum
```

Instead of storing the number values as separate variables they could instead be stored inside an array, depending on the situation. It wouldn't matter if there were 5, 10 or 500 values you wouldn't have to change the sum's expression.

The **reduce** method loops through all the values in the **row** array and returns the result: starting from **0** it adds the current **value** to the **acc** (accumulator), returning the sub-total for the next item in the array.

Now let's say you wanted to show some text in a cell if the value of **F1** was more than 9,000. To do that you would use an IF condition:

fn	=IF(F1 > 9000, "Over", "Under")					
	A	B	C	D	E	F
1	10	20	30	40	50	150
2	Under					

Converting that to JavaScript is easy too:

```
let A2;
if (F1 > 9000) {
  A2 = 'Over';
} else {
  A2 = 'Under';
}
```

Remember that using **let** when declaring the **A2** variable means you can change it *after* it's been declared. If you wanted to do it in a single line, and make it look like the spreadsheet version, you'd use a ternary (this or that) condition:

```
const A2 = F1 > 9000 ? 'Over' : 'Under';
```

This one-liner does the same thing as the longer **if** statement and is fine when you only care about it be one or the other (yes, you can nest them but they can get messy).

How about a spreadsheet like this (with more realistic data):

	A	B	C
1		August	September
2		100	320
3		110	450
4		50	1000
5	Sub total	=SUM(B2:B4)	=SUM(C2:C4)
6		Total	=B5+C5

You could represent the data as an object:

```
const data = {
  august: [100, 110, 50],
  september: [320, 450, 1000],
};
```

With each month's values in an array you can add them together creating their sub-totals and total:

```
const augustSum = data.august.reduce(
  (acc, value) => acc + value,
  0
);
const septemberSum = data.september.reduce(
  (acc, value) => acc + value,
  0
);
const total = augustSum + septemberSum;
```

This allows you to follow the same pattern of having sub-totals for August and September before adding them together. If you just want the total and don't care about the sub-totals:

```
const total = Object.values(data).reduce((acc, month) => {
  const subTotal = acc + month.reduce((acc, value) => {
    return acc + value;
  }, 0);
  return subTotal;
}, 0);
```

Looping with **reduce** through each month, and then the values of that month is an example of a nested loop. As you become more comfortable with loops, functions and programming in general you could remove some extra code, making this:

```
const total = Object.values(data).reduce(
  (acc, month) => acc + month.reduce(
    (acc, value) => acc + value, 0
  ), 0
);
```

It's because of the small amount of code being used in the first place. Take this:

```
const totalLong = row.reduce((acc, value) => {
  return acc + value;
}, 0);
```

This is more about your preferences, but because the **return acc + value** is simple enough to be on a single line (no extra variables to declare or anything like that) then it can be shortened:

```
const totalShort = row.reduce((acc, value) => acc + value, 0);
```

Again though, it's up to you.

Promises

Up until now everything you've seen in JavaScript is synchronous: each line of code is run and then it moves onto the next. If there's a big loop or a task that requires a lot of computation then the thread that JavaScript works on will be locked until it's complete. That's because once-upon-a-time JavaScript ran on computers with less capabilities and keeping it to one thread made things simpler.

Now you still have one thread (for the most part) but now you have Promises. This is a way of telling JavaScript that you want it to run some code but not have it lock the thread. So while everything else runs synchronously you now have a way to run code asynchronously. Why is that useful? If you need to request data from a server you don't want the user interface to suddenly lock until it finishes. Take this example:

```
const getIDs = () => {
  return new Promise((resolve, reject) => {
    setTimeout(() => {
      resolve([832, 883, 432, 1924]);
    }, 1000);
  });
};
getIDs().then((ids) => console.log(ids));
```

The **getIds** function returns a **Promise** with two arguments: **resolve** and **reject**. Inside that is a **setTimeout** function. When the 1 second is up it returns the **ids** using the **resolve** argument. When you call the **getIds** function you can write additional code that is only run when the **Promise** is resolved (**then**). If you want it to fail, you can **reject** it.

```
const getIDs = () => {
  return new Promise((resolve, reject) => {
    setTimeout(() => {
      if (Math.random() < 0.5) {
        reject(new Error('Cannot get IDs')); // <- new
      } else {
        resolve([832, 883, 432, 1924]);
      }
    }, 1000);
  });
};
```

Now there's a good chance it will throw an error. Here's how to **catch** it:

```
getIDs()
  .then((ids) => console.log(ids))
  .catch((error) => console.log(error));
```

If you're dealing with one Promise at a time using **then** and **catch** is fine, but problems start when you begin nesting the calls to async functions. Sometimes you have code that depends on the result of the request. Fortunately, there's a way to fix that. Take this dice rolling function:

```
const rollDice = () => {
  return new Promise((resolve, reject) => {
    setTimeout(() => {
      const role = Math.floor(Math.random() * 6) + 1;
      resolve(role);
    }, 2000);
  });
};
```

And you'd typically use this:

```
rollDice()
  .then(
    (result) => console.log(`You rolled a ${result}`)
  );
```

But you can also use this:

```
const init = async () => {
  const result = await rollDice();
  console.log(`You rolled a ${result}`);
};
init();
```

Now the **rollDice** function has an extra word in front of it: **await**. This can only be used on Promises, and it means the parent function that calls it (**init**) needs to be asynchronous: **async**.

This style has other benefits. If you wanted to roll two die you don't have to nest them like this:

```
rollDice().then((result1) => {
  rollDice().then((result2) => {
    console.log(`You rolled a ${result1} and a ${result2}`);
  });
});
```

Instead you can write it like this:

```
const init = async () => {
  const result1 = await rollDice();
  const result2 = await rollDice();
  console.log(`You rolled a ${result1} and a ${result2}`);
};
init();
```

Which is much cleaner code! And Promises have more benefits. You can use **Promise.all** to run two or more promises at the same time:

```
const init = async () => {
  const [result1, result2] = await Promise.all(
```

```
    [rollDice(), rollDice()]
  );
  console.log(`You rolled a ${result1} and a ${result2}`);
};
init();
```

Promise.all accepts an array of promises and returns the results in
another array. This does have a downside: it expects all the promises to
successfully resolve. If you modify the **rollDice** function to potentially
reject the promise:

```
const rollDice = () => {
  return new Promise((resolve, reject) => {
    setTimeout(() => {
      if (Math.random() < 0.5) {
        reject(new Error('Dropped the dice!')); // <-
      } else {
        const role = Math.ceil(Math.random() * 6);
        resolve(role);
      }
    }, 2000);
  });
};
```

There's a chance rolling the dice will throw an error. When it happens the
console.log you were expecting won't be called. This can be handled by
either wrapping the call with a **try/catch** or using the
Promise.allSettled method:

```
const init = async () => {
  const [result1, result2] = await Promise.allSettled(
    [rollDice(), rollDice()]
  );

  if (result1.status === 'fulfilled' &&
      result2.status === 'fulfilled') {
    console.log(`You rolled a ${result1.value} and a
${result2.value}`);
```

```
  } else {
    console.log('Something went wrong');
  }
};
init();
```

It will allow errors to be thrown but still let the code continue. This can give you more granular control over what to do if a promise fails, like trying again or showing a specific error message.

There's also **Promise.race**:

```
const init = async () => {
  const result = await Promise.race(
    [rollDice(), rollDice()]
  );
  console.log(result);
};
init();
```

This makes two attempts to roll the dice. Whichever one is resolved or rejected first is the value returned to the **result**. There's no second or third place with that method.

Let's ditch the **setTimeout**: the main reason you'll use Promise is when you need to get data from an endpoint:

```
const getData = () => {
  return fetch('https://not-a-real-url.com/users')
    .then((response) => response.json());
};

const init = async () => {
  const users = await getData();
  console.log(users);
};
init();
```

This uses a hybrid of the two approaches. The **init** function **await**s for the promise, but the **getData** function uses the original **then** method of the **fetch** function. This is frequently done to ensure the **response** is

encoded correctly as a JSON object without adding extra bulk to the init function.

And yes, this will fail if you run it with a fake or invalid URL. You can search for 'public endpoints for testing' to get some more useful data endpoints to test if this works.

Promises can also cause problems if you're running them within the normal flow of code. Take this example:

```
const data = [1, 2, 3, 4, 5, 6, 7, 8, 9, 10];

const remove = () => {
  for (let i = 0; i < data.length; i++) {
    data.splice(i, 1);
  }
};

remove();
console.log(data); // [2, 4, 6, 8, 10]
```

The remove function will remove every other number: when the splice is used the array replaces the value of the current index with the value in the next index.

Index	0	1	2	3	4	5	6	7	8	9
Value	1	2	3	4	5	6	7	8	9	10
i = 0	1	2	3	4	5	6	7	8	9	10
i = 1	2	3	4	5	6	7	8	9	10	
i = 2	2	4	5	6	7	8	9	10		
i = 3	2	4	6	7	8	9	10			
i = 4	2	4	6	8	9	10				
data =	2	4	6	8	10					

But if a Promise is added to the loop:

```
const data = [1, 2, 3, 4, 5, 6, 7, 8, 9, 10];
const delay = (ms) => new Promise((resolve) =>
setTimeout(resolve, ms));

const remove = async () => {
```

```
for (let i = 0; i < data.length; i++) {
    await delay(10);
    data.splice(i, 1);
  }
};

remove();
console.log(data); // [1, 2, 3, 4, 5, 6, 7, 8, 9, 10]
```

The **remove** function is still correct but the `delay` in the loop means that the Promise has to wait until it's resolved. This means that the **remove** call needs to have an `await` added before it. You can fix it by wrapping the function in another `async`:

```
const init = async () => {
  await remove();
  console.log(data); // [2, 4, 6, 8, 10]
};

init();
```

If you don't add the `await` and call the **remove** function in the normal flow then the **data** array won't be changed, even though you still had the `console.log(data)` right after it. It would still be pending.

Sorting

You have several folder names you need to sort. They're in an array like this:

```
const data = ['Folder 1', 'Folder 2', 'Folder 3', 'Folder 11',
'Folder 12', 'Folder 10'];
```

No problem, you can use the **sort** method for arrays:

```
data.sort()
```

And here's the result:

```
[ 'Folder 1', 'Folder 10', 'Folder 11', 'Folder 12', 'Folder 2',
'Folder 3' ]
```

Folder 10 is between 1 and 11, which is not what you hoped for. The problem is that the default **sort** method compares each of the values as strings. To see this another way, here is the same array but only with the numbers:

```
const data = [1, 2, 3, 11, 12, 10];
```

And when it's sorted:

```
[ 1, 10, 11, 12, 2, 3 ]
```

By default, the **sort** method compares each value as a string and try to sort them alphabetically. And to sort those strings it convers each character into UTF-16:

Number	UTF-16 value
1	49
10	49, 48
11	49, 49
12	49, 50
2	50
3	51

As strings 1, 10, 11 and 13 occur before 2 and 3: so as far as JavaScript is concerned it did the right thing. To sort the array by numbers you need to add your own compare callback function:

```
data.sort((a, b) => a - b)
```

The **sort** method provides the first value **a** and the second value **b** to be compared:

- If the result of **a** − **b** is a negative then **a** will be ordered before **b**.
- If the result of **a** − **b** is a 0 then the values will stay.
- If the result of **a** − **b** is a positive then **b** will be ordered before **a**.

Back to the array of numbers:

```
const data = [1, 2, 3, 11, 12, 10];
```

1. 1 − 2 = -1 (no change)
2. 2 − 3 = -1 (no change)
3. 3 − 11 = -8 (no change)
4. 11 − 12 = -1 (no change)
5. 12 − 10 = 2 (swap)

And it will keep doing that until there's nothing left to swap:

```
OG: [1, 2, 3, 11, 12, 10]
1st: [1, 2, 3, 11, 10, 12]
2nd: [1, 2, 3, 10, 11, 12]
```

The result of the 2nd pass has nothing left to swap, which means no more 10, 11 and 12 before 2 and 3. That's great for numbers, but not for the original array of folders.

```
const data = ['Folder 1', 'Folder 2', 'Folder 3', 'Folder 11',
'Folder 12', 'Folder 10'];
```

To sort these you need JavaScript to do a little more work before it just compares them as strings. It needs to know there's numbers to sort:

```
const result = data.sort((a, b) =>
  a.localeCompare(b, undefined, { numeric: true })
);
```

The **localeCompare** method – with the *very* important use of the **numeric** option – makes JavaScript consider two things: the first is the current locale, with **undefined** meaning to use whatever the default locale is, and second is that numbers are in the strings and they need to be sorted too.

This gives a much better result:

```
[ 'Folder 1', 'Folder 2', 'Folder 3', 'Folder 10', 'Folder 11',
'Folder 12' ]
```

Sorting for performance

At some point the compare function you use while sorting will hit a problem: as it becomes more complex and the amount of data it has to process grows, so too will the delay. Let's say you have an array of objects that looks like this:

```
const birthdays = [
  {
    name: "John",
    date: "1-1-1995"
  },
  {
    name: "Abby",
    date: "12-10-1998"
  },
  {
    name: "Kim",
    date: "22-2-1992"
  },
  {
    name: "Bob",
    date: "21-8-1997"
  }
];
```

And you need to sort them by their **date**:

```javascript
birthdays.sort((a, b) => {
  // Split the date string into an array
  const [dayA, monthA, yearA] = a.date.split('-');
  const [dayB, monthB, yearB] = b.date.split('-');

  // Re-assemble the date string
  const dateA = new Date(yearA, monthA - 1, dayA);
  const dateB = new Date(yearB, monthB - 1, dayB);

  // Return the difference in milliseconds
  return dateA.getTime() - dateB.getTime();
});
```

You can see in the comments that extra work is needed:

- Each string date needs to be split into day, month and year values
- Those values need to be re-assembled into an actual Date object
- The time value needs to be compared just like before

This is fine for a couple of birthdays, but what happens if you want to sort 100,000 of them? *Every single time* the compare function runs it needs to process the dates. For the array of numbers earlier it went through a few passes before it finished, so how may passes would be needed for that 100,000?

One way to speed this up is to pre-process the compare function. You can add one additional step before sorting:

```javascript
const mapped = birthdays.map((item) => {
  // Split the date string into an array
  const [day, month, year] = item.date.split('-');

  // Re-assemble the date
  const date = new Date(year, month - 1, day);

  // Return the difference in milliseconds
  return {
```

```
  ...item,
  value: date.getTime()
  }
});
```

The returned **mapped** array has added an extra **value** property that you can then use just like before:

```
const sorted = mapped.sort((a, b) => a.value - b.value);
```

Which looks like this:

```
[
  {
    date: "22-2-1992",
    name: "Kim",
    value: 698677200000,
  },
  {
    date: "1-1-1995",
    name: "John",
    value: 788882400000,
  },
  {
    date: "21-8-1997",
    name: "Bob",
    value: 872085600000,
  },
  {
    date: "12-10-1998",
    name: "Abby",
    value: 908114400000,
  },
];
```

Now let's see it work with more data. First, let's generate 100,000 birthdays (the **date** is an array of random values joined with a hyphen to create a string):

```
const birthdays = Array(100000)
  .fill()
  .map((_, i) => ({
    name: `Person ${i}`,
    date: [
      Math.floor(Math.random() * 28),
      Math.floor(Math.random() * 12),
      1990 + Math.floor(Math.random() * 20),
    ].join("-"),
  }));
```

And then test the two methods in a benchmark to see which is faster:

```
const regularSort = () => {
  birthdays.sort((a, b) => {
    // Split the date string into an array
    const [dayA, monthA, yearA] = a.date.split('-');
    const [dayB, monthB, yearB] = b.date.split('-');

    // Re-assemble the date string
    const dateA = new Date(yearA, monthA - 1, dayA);
    const dateB = new Date(yearB, monthB - 1, dayB);

    // Return the difference in milliseconds
    return dateA.getTime() - dateB.getTime();
  });
};

const mappedSort = () => {
  const mapped = birthdays.map((item) => {
    // Split the date string into an array
    const [day, month, year] = item.date.split('-');

    // Re-assemble the date
    const date = new Date(year, month - 1, day);

    // Return the difference in milliseconds
```

```
  return {
    ...item,
    value: date.getTime(),
  };
});
mapped.sort((a, b) => a.value - b.value);
};

// Add tests
const suite = new Benchmark.Suite();
suite
  .add('regularSort', regularSort)
  .add('mappedSort', mappedSort)
  .on('cycle', function (event) {
    console.log(String(event.target));
  })
  .on('complete', function () {
    console.log('Fastest is ' +
this.filter('fastest').pluck('name'));
  })
  .run({ async: true });
```

The results are in, and…

- regularSort x 13.99 operations per second
- mappedSort x 18.78 operations per second

The fastest is the **mappedSort** function. Both functions were still very fast, but more complex comparisons will take longer. The **mappedSort** function also gives you the option to process other parts of each object, like calculating the number of days until each person's next birthday.

Proxy

Objects let you store data as key/value pairs. But what if you wanted to check something because they were set, or validate the values whenever they're changed? A Proxy is like wrapping an object in extra code that allows you to control what happens during the **get** and **set** process.

Let's say you declare an object, do some other things, then set the values:

```
const person = {};

// more code here

person.name = ' John Doe   ';
person.age = '32';
```

The **name** value has some extra spaces and the **age** really should be a number. If you know others are going to work on this after you (and that *includes* you after working on several other products), it would be a good idea to spare them some pain and validate these values. But if you know these will be set across multiple locations in your code, then letting the object validate itself might be the way to go.

You can start with this:

```
const validator = {
  set: function (obj, prop, value) {
    let result = value;
```

```
    // ...more code here

    obj[prop] = result;
  }
};
```

Your new **validator** object has a **set** function, and you'll also see **obj**, **prop** and **value** as arguments. If the **prop** is **name**, then you can run some checks:

```
const validator = {
  set: function (obj, prop, value) {
    let result = value;
    switch (prop) {
      case 'name':
        if (typeof result !== 'string') {
          throw new TypeError('The name is not a string');
        }
        break;
    }

    obj[prop] = result;
  }
};
```

This will enable the object to check that the value you're trying to **set** is a string. To make the **validator** manage the object:

```
const person = new Proxy({}, validator);
person.name = ' John Doe ';
```

The **Proxy** accepts two arguments: an object and the handler (in this case the **validator**). To remove the extra spaces before the **name** is **set** just update the handler to **trim** the **result**:

```
        if (typeof result !== 'string') {
          throw new TypeError('The name is not a string');
        }
```

```
        result = result.trim(); // <- new
        break;
```

You can also add a condition for the **age** to check if it's a number:

```
    case 'age':
        if (!Number.isInteger(result)) {
            throw new TypeError('The age is not an integer');
        }
        break;
```

Now it will throw an error before setting the **age**. And this isn't limited to just setting the value – you can do the same when getting them:

```
get: function (obj, prop) {
    if (prop === 'age' && obj[prop] > 120) {
        console.log('Over 120 years old? Really?');
    }

    return obj[prop];
}
```

In this example it will still return the **age**, but will also show a message. You can also take it further by changing the returned values:

```
get: function (obj, prop) {
    if (prop === 'age' && obj[prop] > 120) {
        console.log('Over 120 years old? Really?');
    }
    if (prop === 'name') {
        return (obj[prop] || '').toUpperCase();
    }

    return obj[prop];
}
```

Now when you do this:

```
console.log(person.name); // JOHN DOE
```

The **name** has been converted into uppercase characters (and no extra spaces before and after). Now if/when you need to show the **name** later you won't have to worry about trimming it.

Recursion

Before you move into the advanced stuff it's a good idea to understand recursion in JavaScript. The simplest explanation for recursion is when a function can call itself, like this:

```
const showMessage = () => {
  console.log('Hello world!');
  showMessage();
};
```

Running that example is a bad idea, not because it's recursion but because it has nothing to *stop it*. There's no counter to be used in a condition to stop it like a loop, no timer to make is run for 300 milliseconds, nothing. Your browser will eventually stop it by giving you a warning but this is a quick way to become frustrated.

If you need a function to call itself then that's fine, just make sure it knows when to stop. Several functions in the next chapter have elements of recursion, but you're going to use a more useful form of it here.

Let's say you have some data in an object:

```
const data = {
  name: 'Alex',
  age: 30,
  details: {
    sport: 'Cycling',
```

```
    work: 'Engineer'
  }
};
```

Recursion can be used to read each of those:

```
const traverseJSON = (obj) => {
  for (let key in obj) {
    if (typeof obj[key] === 'object' &&
        obj[key] !== null) {
      console.log(`Key: ${key}`);
      traverseJSON(obj[key]);
    } else {
      console.log(`Key: ${key}, Value: ${obj[key]}`);
    }
  }
};
```

And to traverse the **data** you call the function with the **data** as an argument:

```
traverseJSON(data);
```

A **for** loop goes through each **key** in the object. If the value is another object then the **traverseJSON** function is called again to continue the loop. This will output:

```
Key: name, Value: Alex
Key: age, Value: 30
Key: details
Key: sport, Value: Cycling
Key: work, Value: Engineer
```

Quickly check this line:

```
traverseJSON(obj[key]);
```

If you used **obj** instead of **obj[key]** you'd have the same problem as the **showMessage** example: it would just keep looping.

Because of the way the **data** is structured the recursion will eventually stop: there's only one nested object (**details**) so it won't go any further. Even if there were more nested objects it will still stop the recursion when there are no more objects to parse.

Traversing the **data** is great, but what if you needed something more targeted? What if you wanted to find a value in the data?

```
const findValue = (obj, value) => {
  for (let key in obj) {
    if (typeof obj[key] === 'object' &&
        obj[key] !== null) {
      const result = findValue(obj[key], value);
      if (result) {
        return true;
      }
    } else if (obj[key] === value) {
      return true;
    }
  }
  return false;
}

console.log(findValue(data, 'Cycling')); // true
console.log(findValue(data, 'Tennis')); // false
```

The structure is similar to the **traverseJSON** function, but now there's the **value** argument and it returns a boolean if it finds a matching value. Let's see how this works:

- key = name, value = Alex (does not equal Cycling)
- key = age, value = 30 (does not equal Cycling)
- key = details
  o key = sport, value = Cycling (matches)
    ▪ return true

In this example the **data** is processed as the object is traversed but the returned value is passed back up: it's sent all the way back to become the value of **findValue**. And if you wanted to find if a key exists:

```
const findKey = (obj, key) => {
  for (let objKey in obj) {
    if (objKey === key) {
      return true;
    }
    if (typeof obj[objKey] === 'object' &&
        obj[objKey] !== null) {
      const result = findKey(obj[objKey], key);
      if (result) {
        return true;
      }
    }
  }
  return false;
}

console.log(findKey(data, 'sport'));   // true
console.log(findKey(data, 'address')); // false
```

But what if you wanted to trace the object keys, kind of like creating a breadcrumb trail for your data?

```
const findKeyPath = (obj, key, path = []) => {
  for (let objKey in obj) {
    if (objKey === key) {
      path.push(key);
      return path;
    }
    if (typeof obj[objKey] === 'object' &&
        obj[objKey] !== null) {
      const result = findKeyPath(obj[objKey], key,
path.concat(objKey));
      if (result) {
        return result;
      }
    }
  }
  return false;
```

```
}

console.log(findKeyPath(data, 'sport'));
// ['details', 'sport']
console.log(findKeyPath(data, 'address'));
// false
```

The **findKeyPath** function does just that: give it the **key** you're looking for and instead of telling you if it exists it will return the trail of keys it traversed to find the one you wanted.

But recursion isn't the only way to traverse an object. First let's make the **data** a little more complicated:

```
const data = {
  name: 'Alex',
  age: 30,
  details: {
    sport: 'Cycling',
    work: 'Engineer',
    orders: [
      {
        id: 1,
        item: 'Item 1'
      },
      {
        id: 2,
        item: 'Item 2'
      }
    ]
  }
};
```

Now check this out:

```
const findByPath = (obj, path) => {
  const keys = path.split('.');
  let result = obj;
  keys.forEach((key) => {
```

```
    if (!result ||
        typeof result !== 'object' ||
        !result[key]) {
      result = undefined;
    }
    result = result[key];
  });
  return result;
};

console.log(findByPath(data, 'details.sport'));
// 'Cycling'
console.log(findByPath(data, 'details.orders.1.item'));
// 'Item 2'
console.log(findByPath(data, 'details.orders.2.item')); //
undefined
```

The **findByPath** function doesn't use recursion in the traditional way. Using the **path** argument it changes the value of the **result** variable as it loops through each of the **keys**. You have to check and make sure the newly changed **result** is a valid object to parse, but it might be a better option for some situations.

Known issues

JavaScript has some quirks. Before 1995 pages on the internet were entirely static[2]. No AJAX (Asynchronous JavaScript and XML) requests, frameworks or real-time updating of content. While there were Java applets that could add dynamic elements to a page there was a lack of a scripting language that could bridge the HTML elements with the Java applets.

So a scripting language was created and named JavaScript. It required no compiler, was high level (making it very easy to learn), used dynamic typing and 'just worked' for those who tried it. No wonder it became so popular!

Types and equality

But it came with some quirks. The dynamically typed variables and 'just work' mindset meant it would do some unusual things, even in 2024. Earlier you learned about Boolean variables and how they represent **true** and **false**, or **1** and **0**. Here's proof:

```
console.log(true == 1); // true
```

2

https://web.archive.org/web/20070916144913/https://wp.netscape.com/newsref/pr/new
srelease67.html

Which means that:

```
console.log(true + true); // 2
```

On its own that's not a major issue. But this is:

```
console.log(1 + '1'); // '11'
```

Rather than throw an error JavaScript tries to resolve this. It can't add a string to a number, so it converts the number to a string and concatenates it. And it gets a little stranger if you try to reverse it:

```
console.log('11' - 1); // 10
```

So it's important that you know what values you're working with before you use them. Languages like TypeScript can help with that and give you warnings if/when they're wrong. But there have been some improvements since JavaScript was first built. You can use an equality check. Remember this?

```
console.log(true == 1); // true
```

Adding an extra = checks both the value and the type:

```
console.log(true === 1); // false
```

A lot of the time you'll see === used more often than == because it prevents problems with equality.

Floating point numbers

```
console.log(1 + 2); // 3
console.log(0.1 + 0.2); // 0.30000000000000004
```

The numbers are fine. It's an issue with how JavaScript handles arithmetic, specifically with floating point numbers: when it's read by the browser for addition the numbers are converted into binary.

There are no perfect representations of 0.1 and 0.2, so what you get is an approximation. This isn't unique to JavaScript either: Java, Python, C,

PHP and other languages that use the IEEE 754[3] standard for floating numbers do this too.

32-bit numbers

There are some hacks that you can use in JavaScript to simplify your code. Let's say you have a number and you want to remove the decimal places:

```
const num = 123456789.012
console.log(parseInt(num)); // 123456789
```

The **parseInt** function will do the job nicely. But there are other ways you remove the decimal places:

```
console.log(num | 0); // 123456789
console.log(~~num); // 123456789
console.log(num >> 0); // 123456789
```

They all return the same: **123456789**. But there's a minor/major issue depending on how you use them that you need to know. JavaScript numbers are usually 64-bit numbers, but those last three lines convert them to 32-bit numbers. That becomes a problem here:

```
const today = new Date('2037-01-20T00:00:01.1Z');
const timestamp = today.getTime() / 1000;
const shifted = ~~timestamp;
const newDate = new Date(shifted * 1000);
console.log(newDate.toISOString()); // 2037-01-20T00:00:01.000Z
```

This takes a date that has seconds and milliseconds (the **01.1**) and removes them using the ~~ operator before converting it back to a date. But if you change the date to the following year:

```
const today = new Date('2038-01-20T00:00:01.1Z');
```

---

[3] https://en.wikipedia.org/wiki/IEEE_754

You get:

```
1901-12-14T17:31:45.000Z
```

You've just caused a bug. This only impacts those times when a number is converted to 32-bits because they can't go that high – remember that JavaScript stores dates as timestamps. The largest 32-bit number is 2,147,483,647 so when the timestamp is converted to seconds and the bitwise ~~ hack is used, you've just converted the 20th of January, 2038 to the 14th of December, 1901:

```
2037-01-20T00:00:01.1Z / 1000 = 2116022401.1
~~2116022401.1 = 2116022401

2038-01-20T00:00:01.1Z / 1000 = 2147558401.1
~~2147558401.1 = -2147408895
```

If you're working with a legacy codebase you might see similar hacks when working with numbers created by other engineers. Using `parseInt(timestamp)` would have prevented the sudden change in the data and could be valuable if you start to notice problems in 2038.

Intermediate projects

You've learned the basics, so it's time to start on some projects. These will help you apply what you've just learned in various ways and reinforce that knowledge. If *anything* you read in the following pages gives you ideas of future JavaScript projects then that's great! Stop reading this book right now and give it a try. Otherwise keep reading and see if you're inspired by something else.

Each of these projects are built to help you use your newfound JavaScript knowledge. But don't view them as the only way to do it. As your skills develop you'll want to try different things, and feel free to do so, but if you get stuck then take a break before checking what you wrote. You'd be surprised how a single character might cause you problems, which is why working in an Integrated Development Environment (IDE) is a good idea. They can help you find issues before quickly.

Another thing to know is that while creating this book, each project's code was developed through iteration. They all started with fragments of code that were written, merged and changed over time. None of them 'just happened', and yes, there were a lot of iterations before these were finished.

Fizz Buzz

The Fizz Buzz game is used to help teach children about numbers, specifically if one number is divisible by another. A child in a group starts counting from 1 and each child takes turns saying the next number, except for when that number is a multiple of 3 or 5. On those numbers, the child would say 'fizz' instead of saying 3, 6, and 9, 'buzz' for 5, 10 and 20. When a child gets to a number that is a multiple of both 3 and 5 (like 15, 30 and 45) they say 'fizz buzz'.

So let's rework the Fizz Buzz game into something more code friendly:

Create a list of Fizz Buzz answers for the numbers 1 to 100. If the number is a multiple of 3, write "Fizz". If it's a multiple of 5, write "Buzz". But if it's a multiple of 3 and 5, write "FizzBuzz". For anything else just write the number.

Before you can write this in *any* programming language you need to understand the requirements of what you're being asked to do, or simply asking 'What?':

- What are the minimum and maximum numbers?
- What would the first 10 numbers look like?
- What about the next 10?

No code has been written yet and that's intentional. Writing code is easy, but if you don't understand the problem then your code won't successfully solve the it. The next thing you need to ask yourself is 'How?':

- How do you list those numbers?
- How will the code know when to stop?
- How will you check if the numbers are multiples of 3 or 5?

Starting with the last one first: you can check if one number is a multiple of another using the modulo operator: **%**. Let's check out how you could find out if a number is even:

```
const even = (n) => n % 2 === 0;
```

Your number (**n**) is divided by 2 however modulo returns the remainder, so:

- **4 % 2 = 0** (4 ÷ 2 = 2, no remainder) and,
- **5 % 2 = 5** (5 ÷ 2 = 2.5)
  - o 5 is the remainder

This function also includes an equality check (**===**): it's looking to see if the result/remainder of the modulo operator equals 0. If it does then the function returns a value of **true** (because 2 *is a multiple of* 4), otherwise it returns **false**.

Back to the other 'Hows'. Listing them and knowing when to stop: that's going to be a loop. When you're working with a sequence of numbers where each of them needs to be tested then a loop is your best bet:

```
for (let i = 1; i <= 100; ++i) {
  // more to come
}
```

This loop starts at **1**, is incremented by 1 every time it loops (**++1**) and stops when it gets to **100**. Now you need your loop to do something:

```
for (let i = 1; i <= 100; ++i) {
  console.log(i);
}
```

When this loop runs it will print out your list of numbers from 1 to 100. That's great, but there's more it needs to do. There are conditions that need to be written just like the **even** function from before:

```
for (let i = 1; i <= 100; ++i) {
  if (i % 3 === 0) {
    console.log('Fizz');
  } else {
    console.log(i);
  }
}
```

The **i % 3 === 0** is the same structure that was used for the **even** function. And just like before this will return **true** or **false** depending on the value of **i**.

What's new is the **if/else** statement. The only thing **if/else** statements care about are whether the value between the first and last parenthesis is **true**, and if it is then it does what's inside. If it's **false** then it moves on.

The loop checks if the value is a multiple of 3 and prints out 'Fizz', otherwise it prints out the number. Now add the check for multiples of 5:

```
for (let i = 1; i <= 100; ++i) {
  if (i % 3 === 0) {
    console.log('Fizz');
  } else if (i % 5 === 0) {
    console.log('Buzz');
  } else {
    console.log(i);
  }
}
```

Congratulations! Your loop can now do 'Fizz' and 'Buzz'. Does it feel like you missed something? What about 'FizzBuzz'? You might think adding another condition would be the next step, like this:

```
for (let i = 1; i <= 100; ++i) {
  if (i % 3 === 0) {
    console.log('Fizz');
  } else if (i % 5 === 0) {
    console.log('Buzz');
```

```
} else if (i % 3 === 0 && i % 5 === 0) {
  console.log('FizzBuzz');
} else {
  console.log(i);
}
}
```

And this is what the first 14 numbers would look like:

```
1
2
Fizz
4
Buzz
Fizz
7
8
Fizz
Buzz
11
Fizz
13
14
```

15 would print out 'FizzBuzz', right? Unfortunately, it won't get that chance. The order of operations means it will perform the 'is it a multiple of 3' check and succeed because 15 is a multiple of 3, so it will never get to the other checks.

You could reorder the conditions to check if the 3 and 5 combo occurs first, but there's another way:

```
for (let i = 1; i <= 100; ++i) {
  let output = '';
  if (i % 3 === 0) output += 'Fizz';
  if (i % 5 === 0) output += 'Buzz';
  console.log(output || i);
}
```

This loop does the same thing, except it's using string concatenation to give the results (concatenation is like adding/appending one string to another: '1' + '1' equals '11'). At the start of every loop the output variable is declared as an empty string. When it does its check for multiples of 3 it concatenates 'Fizz' to the empty string variable if it's true, but if it's false it moves on to the next 'Buzz' check.

When the number is 15, 30, 45 or another multiple of 3 and 5 both checks return true, so both 'Fizz' and 'Buzz' are concatenated together.

The final part occurs in the console.log. This is another kind of condition using the OR operator ||. Basically: return the output if it has a value, otherwise return the number. If the checks don't concatenate anything to the output, then it will print the number.

And this is what the new 15 looks like:

```
1
2
Fizz
4
Buzz
Fizz
7
8
Fizz
Buzz
11
Fizz
13
14
FizzBuzz
```

There are other ways of writing this too. Here's one if you prefer arrays:

```javascript
for (let i = 1; 1 <= 100; ++i) {
  const output = [];
  if (i % 3 === 0) output.push('Fizz');
  if (i % 5 === 0) output.push('Buzz');
  console.log(output.join('') || i);
}
```

Or template literals, but it's not the most readable option:

```
for (let i = 1; i <= 100; ++i) {
  console.log(`${i % 3 === 0 ? 'Fizz' : ''}${i % 5 === 0 ? 'Buzz'
: ''}` || i);
}
```

Whatever option you choose your code should now give you a full list of answers.

Loot boxes

A new client has asked you to create a basic mechanic for their new game – a loot box – an award that gives a prize based on probability. But first they want proof that it will give the expected results. When the function to determine what kind of prize is generated it needs to use the following:

- 50% chance of a common item
- 30% chance of a rare item
- 15% chance of an epic item
- 5% chance of a legendary item

You know already that you need to work with random numbers so `Math.random()` will be part of the function. As for the 'percent chance' of an item?

```
const makePrize = () => {
  const random = Math.random();

  if (random < 0.5) {
    return 'common';
  } else if (random < 0.8) {
    return 'rare';
  } else if (random < 0.95) {
    return 'epic';
  } else {
```

```
    return 'legendary';
  }
};
```

The 50% is the least value (common) so that can be used as a starting point for the conditions. Each condition that follows builds on that initial `0.5`:

- `0.5 + 0.3 = 0.8`
- `0.8 + 0.15 = 0.95`
- `0.95 + 0.05 = 1.0`

And now you need to prove it.

```
const lootBoxTest = (n) => {
  const loot = {};
  for (let i = 0; i < n; i++) {
    const prize = makePrize();
    loot[prize] = loot[prize] ? loot[prize] + 1 : 1;
  }
  return loot;
};

console.log(lootBoxTest(1000));
```

The **lootBoxTest** function simulates 1000 prizes being generated and counts the number of times they occur. Random numbers will generate random results, but you should see values similar to this:

`{ common: 514, rare: 271, epic: 184, legendary: 31 }`

Prior to accepting the work, you did some due diligence on the client and found they have a history of creating free apps and games with a paid element (freemium). You ask the question and yes, they would like another kind of loot box that has an optional token/key/coin the player can use to get a better item.

First, you need to add an argument to the **makePrize** function so it can support the paid version:

```
const makePrize = (paid = false) => {
```

The second change needed is to add the new chances (between the declaration of the **random** variable and the original conditions:

```
const random = Math.random(); // <- original

if (paid) {
  if (random < 0.5) {
    return 'rare';
  } else if (random < 0.75) {
    return 'epic';
  } else {
    return 'legendary';
  }
}

if (random < 0.5) { // <- original
```

You next change involves supporting the **paid** argument in the **lootBoxTest** function:

```
const lootBoxTest = (n, paid) => {
  const loot = {};
  for (let i = 0; i < n; i++) {
    const prize = makePrize(paid);
    loot[prize] = loot[prize] ? loot[prize] + 1 : 1;
  }
  return loot;
};
```

And finally a new **console.log** to show the output to compare the two versions:

```
console.log(lootBoxTest(1000));
console.log(lootBoxTest(1000, true));
```

Your results will look similar to this:

```
{ common: 479, rare: 306, epic: 170, legendary: 45 }
        { rare: 476, epic: 277, legendary: 247 }
```

Perfect: the paid-version of the loot box now excludes common items and has a greater chance of spawning rare, epic and legendary items. Your client is pleased!

Password strength

We all know what it's like to have to think of a new password when creating an account on a site. Or those situations where you need to reset your password because you forgot it. And they always come with rules, like not using common words, a minimum of 8 characters with a combination of letters, numbers, spaces and special characters.

The reason, whether it's because the site has done their research or is just blindly following everyone else, mostly comes down to password strength: the higher the strength the less likely your password can be guessed using brute-force (though every site should have rate limits on authentication endpoints to prevent that). There's an XKCD[4] comic worth checking out.

Look at these passwords:

```
const passwords = [
  'password',
  'password123',
  'password123!',
  'Tr0ub4dor&3',
  'correcthorsebatterystaple'
];
```

The first three fall under the 'never' category when it comes to passwords as they're too easy to guess. The last two come from the comic.

---

[4] https://xkcd.com/936/

So how can they be tested to see how strong they are? By calculating their entropy. The first **password** is all lowercase letters, which means the range of potential characters is 26 (a to z). The second adds some extra complexity with the addition of numbers, so the range for that one is 35: a to z (25) plus 0 to 9 (10). When you know the potential range of characters you can use this formula to calculate the entropy:

$$Entropy = log_2(R^L)$$

Where R is the range of potential characters in the password and L is the length of the password. Time to write the function:

```javascript
const calculateEntropy = (password) => {
  let n = 0;

  if (password.match(/[0-9]/)) n += 10; // numbers
  if (password.match(/[a-zA-Z]/)) n += 52; // letters
  if (password.match(/[^a-zA-Z0-9]/)) n += 33; // special chars

  return Math.log2(Math.pow(n, password.length));
};
```

This performs three matches and adds numbers to the **n** variable: 10 if there are numbers in the password, 52 if there are letters (26 upper and 26 lower) and 33 if there are special characters (like % or &). Once that's done it returns the result of the entropy formula from before.

Now to see what the entropy of each of those passwords are:

```javascript
passwords.forEach((password) => {
  const entropy = calculateEntropy(password);
  console.log(password, entropy);
});
```

- password 45.603517745128734
- password123 65.49615941425563
- password123! 78.83826729997138
- Tr0ub4dor&3 72.26841169164042
- correcthorsebatterystaple 142.5109929535273

An entropy of 60 is supposed to be good, but because **password123** is so common it's a bad one to use. Adding extra characters helps but again, still not a good choice. The last two passwords scored very highly. The final one in particular only used lowercase letters but because of the length its entropy is stronger than the one viewed as best practice. Keep in mind that combining words is not ideal as it means that others can combine words to brute force it too.

So how many attempts would it take to brute force a password?

```javascript
const potentialAttempts = (entropy) => Math.pow(2, entropy);
```

As long as you know the entropy then getting the number of attempts is fairly easy (for a machine anyway). You can also add this to your loop to see the results:

```javascript
passwords.forEach((password) => {
  const entropy = calculateEntropy(password);
  const attempts = potentialAttempts(entropy);
  console.log(password, entropy, attempts);
});
```

But how can you be sure this is correct? By brute forcing it yourself. Let's say you knew someone was using a four-digit PIN as their password and you wanted to prove it could be cracked (using that as proof that they should change it). You would need to generate all the four-digit combinations:

```javascript
const crackPassword = (count) => {
  const chars = '1234567890';
  const { length: charCount } = chars;
  const passwords = [];

  // Generate all possible passwords
  for (let i = 0; i < Math.pow(charCount, count); i++) {
    let password = '';
    for (let j = 0; j < count; j++) {
      password += chars.charAt(
        Math.floor(i / Math.pow(charCount, j)) % charCount
      );
    }
    passwords.push(password);
```

```
    }

    return passwords;
};
```

This function assumes that you're only going to use numbers. The `Math.pow(charCount, count)` determines the potential number of passwords:

Type	Character range	Password length	Potential number of passwords
Numbers only	10	4	10,000
Lowercase letters	26	8	208,827,064,576
Upper and lowercase letters	52	8	53,459,728,531,456

Go back to your **passwords** array and add the worst four-digit PIN:

```
const passwords = [
    '1234', // <- new password
    'password',
```

The entropy for 1234 is 13.2877 with 9999.99 potential attempts, which is pretty accurate according to the values in the table. Now generate those passwords and return the length to confirm the function is working:

```
const possiblePasswords = crackPassword(4);
console.log(possiblePasswords.length);
```

Generating the 10,000 passwords won't take long, but if you want to see the list it's strongly recommended you look at it in batches:

```
console.log(possiblePasswords.slice(0, 20));
```

As you can see:

```
[ '1111', '2111', '3111', '4111', '5111',
  '6111', '7111', '8111', '9111', '0111',
  '1211', '2211', '3211', '4211', '5211',
  '6211', '7211', '8211', '9211', '0211' ]
```

You now proven that the entropy information is correct. If you wanted to go further you could calculate how long it would take to crack each password. If rate limiting was disabled you could try a password every millisecond:

```
passwords.forEach((password) => {
  const entropy = calculateEntropy(password);
  const attempts = potentialAttempts(entropy);
  const daysToCrack = attempts / (1000 * 60 * 60 * 24);
  console.log(password, entropy, attempts, daysToCrack);
});
```

The four-digit PIN would be cracked very quickly, and while the other passwords would still take time they will break eventually. Again, rate limiting helps to prevent this problem but it's still a good idea to change passwords regularly and make sure you're not sharing them with anyone.

Roman numerals

Given their limitations – no value for 0 and can't really go beyond 3,999 unless you add an overline – showing Roman numerals is still popular. Clocks, book chapters, sports games and copyright dates in film credits all use them, so having a script convert to and from Roman numerals still has value.

Your client wants the current year to be in Roman numerals. To start:

```
const values = {
  M: 1000,
  CM: 900,
  D: 500,
  CD: 400,
  C: 100,
  XC: 90,
  L: 50,
  XL: 40,
  X: 10,
  IX: 9,
  V: 5,
  IV: 4,
  I: 1
};
```

You'll be able to use this for the conversions (as of 2024 there's no native JavaScript that has these values so you need to write them yourself). You might notice a pattern with 1, 4, 5 and 9 and how many zeroes appear after them. There are ways to go beyond 3,999 – because there's no symbol for 5,000 which means you can't write 4,000 – but for most uses it's not necessary.

To convert a decimal number to Roman numerals:

```javascript
const toRoman = (value) => {
  const result = [];

  if (isNaN(value)) {
    throw new Error('Value must be a number');
  }

  if (value < 1) {
    throw new Error('Number must be greater than 0');
  }

  Object.entries(values).forEach(([key, val]) => {
    while (value >= val) {
      result.push(key);
      value -= val;
    }
  });

  return result.join('');
};
```

The first half checks to make sure that the `value` argument is a number greater than 0. The other half is where a conversion happens. If the current `value` is greater than or equal to the `key/val` pair in the loop then the `val` should be subtracted from the `value` and the `key` should be added to the `result`.

For 2024 it looks like this:

Current value	While	Result
2024	2024 >= 1000	M
1024	1024 >= 1000	MM
24	24 >= 10	MMX
14	14 >= 10	MMXX
4	4 >= 4	MMXXIV

```
console.log(toRoman(2024)); // MMXXIV
```

Reversing that is very similar, but instead of a number as the `value` argument you need to use a string.

```
const toDecimal = (value) => {
  let result = 0;

  if (typeof value !== 'string') {
    throw new Error('Value must be a string');
  }

  if (value.length < 1) {
    throw new Error('Value must not be empty');
  }

  Object.entries(values).forEach(([key, val]) => {
    while (value.indexOf(key) === 0) {
      result += val;
      value = value.replace(key, '');
    }
  });

  return result;
};
```

Again the first half are checks to make sure the argument is valid. The `forEach` loop is also similar, except for each `key/val` pair in the `values` object you need to check if its index in the string is 0. If it is then you add the `val` to the `result` and remove the symbol.

Current value	While	Result
MMXXIV	key === 'M'	1000
MXXIV	key === 'M'	2000
XXIV	key === 'X'	2010
XIV	key === 'X'	2020
IV	key === 'IV'	2024

```
console.log(toRoman(2024)); // MMXXIV
```

If you want to write a test to make 100% sure it's going to work for you, then start by creating some test values:

```
const testValues = [1, 2, 3, 4, 5, 39, 2024, 3999, 1009, 1066, 1776, 1918];
```

And then a quick loop to take each of those values, convert them to Roman numerals and then back to decimals:

```
testValues.forEach((value) => {
  const roman = toRoman(value);
  const decimal = toDecimal(roman);
  console.log(
    `${value} => ${roman} => ${decimal}`,
    value === decimal ? '✅' : '❌'
  );
});
```

You should get these results:

- 1 => I => 1 ✅
- 2 => II => 2 ✅
- 3 => III => 3 ✅
- 4 => IV => 4 ✅
- 5 => V => 5 ✅
- 39 => XXXIX => 39 ✅
- 2024 => MMXXIV => 2024 ✅
- 3999 => MMMCMXCIX => 3999 ✅
- 1009 => MIX => 1009 ✅

- `1066 => MLXVI => 1066` ✅
- `1776 => MDCCLXXVI => 1776` ✅
- `1918 => MCMXVIII => 1918` ✅

And there you have it: two reliable functions to handle converting to and from Roman numerals.

The Monty Hall problem

You're invited up to a stage that has three closed doors. The host tells you that one of the doors has a massive cash prize behind them, while the other two have goats. You choose a door but before it's opened the host opens one of the other doors to reveal a goat. You're told you can keep your original choice (stay) or choose the other unopened door (switch). What should you do?

When people try to solve the Monty Hall problem they usually rely on probability and statistics. You're an engineer, so simulating this is your preferred method. You want to follow the same steps as the original game, so time to make some doors:

```
const getDoors = () => {
  const doors = ['goat', 'goat', 'goat'];
  doors[Math.floor(Math.random() * doors.length)] = 'cash';
  return doors;
};
```

If you call the **getDoors** function it will return an array contains three values: two 'goats' and one 'cash' which is randomly selected. You'll be making your choice soon, but first you need to write a function for the host:

```
const hostChooseDoor = (doors, choice) => {
  const altDoor = doors.findIndex(
    (door, i) => door === 'goat' && i !== choice
```

```
);
  return altDoor;
};
```

The host knows what's behind each of the doors so when you've made your choice, they'll pick one of the doors that have a goat behind it. Same thing needs to happen here: the door index that is returned needs to be a goat, not the cash or your choice.

Now for the final decision:

```
const chooseFinalDoor = (doors, original, alt, stay) => {
  if (stay) {
    return original;
  }
  return doors.findIndex(
    (_, i) => i !== original && i !== alt
  );
};
```

If you decide to stay, then your original choice should be returned. Otherwise you need to find the index of the remaining item in the array: it won't be the original or the alternate door the host chose.

Now to simulate the actions:

```
const simulate = (attempts, stay) => {
  let wins = 0;
  let losses = 0;

  console.log(stay ? 'Stay' : 'Switch');
  console.log(` - Wins: ${wins}, Losses: ${losses}`);
};

simulate(1000, true);
simulate(1000, false);
```

More will be added to the **simulate** function, but for now this is fine. This will enable you to run 1,000 attempts of the game and output the results: how many wins (you choose the door with the cash prize) or losses (you picked the goats) based on where you choose to stay or switch your door.

If you're going to test for multiple attempts, then you're going to need a loop:

```
let losses = 0;

for (let i = 0; i < attempts; i++) {
}

console.log(stay ? 'Stay' : 'Switch');
```

And now to fill that loop with the logic needed to test the attempt:

```
for (let i = 0; i < attempts; i++) {
  const doors = getDoors();
  const choice = Math.floor(Math.random() * doors.length);
  const altDoor = hostChooseDoor(doors, choice);
  const newChoice = chooseFinalDoor(doors, choice, altDoor,
stay);

  if (doors[newChoice] === 'cash') {
    ++wins;
  } else {
    ++losses;
  }
}
```

1. You need to get the **doors** using the **getDoors** function from earlier.
2. Randomly choose which door you want to pick.
3. Have the host choose an alternate door.
4. Switch or Stay, depending on the function's **stay** argument.

If the **newChoice** returns **cash**, increment the **wins** variable, otherwise do the same to the **losses** variable. This will count the number of wins and losses which you can use to determine which choice is better.

Here's the full **simulate** function:

```
const simulate = (attempts, stay) => {
  let wins = 0;
```

```
  let losses = 0;

  for (let i = 0; i < attempts; i++) {
    const doors = getDoors();
    const choice = Math.floor(Math.random() * doors.length);
    const altDoor = hostChooseDoor(doors, choice);
    const newChoice = chooseFinalDoor(doors, choice, altDoor,
stay);

    if (doors[newChoice] === 'cash') {
      ++wins;
    } else {
      ++losses;
    }
  }

  console.log(stay ? 'Stay' : 'Switch');
  console.log(` - Wins: ${wins}, Losses: ${losses}`);
};
```

When you run the code it will output results similar to this:

```
Stay
 - Wins: 337, Losses: 663
Switch
 - Wins: 676, Losses: 324
```

If you want to simulate more you can increase the number of attempts when you call the **simulate** function, but according to the results you're more likely to win if you switch doors.

The Numbers Game

There is a game called the Numbers Game (created by Armand Jammot). A contestant is given a choice of numbers that will be used in the game: large or small. The large numbers are 25, 50, 75 and 100 while the small numbers are 1, 2, 3 and all the way to 10. They might say '1 large, 5 small' and as a result 1 of the large numbers will be drawn from the deck and 5 of the small numbers will also be drawn.

- 75, 2, 6, 8, 1, 3

A random number is then picked, called the 'target'. All of the contestants must then calculate that target number using *all* of the drawn cards and *only* those cards (so you can't use the same card multiple times unless it was drawn multiple times).

- 75, 2, 6, 8, 1, 3
- Target is 897

You've been asked to re-create this game for an app. You can start by listing the big and small numbers, their counts and the available operators:

```
const bigNumbers = [25, 50, 75, 100];
const smallNumbers = [1, 2, 3, 4, 5, 6, 7, 8, 9, 10];

const bigCount = 1;
```

```
const smallCount = 5;

const operators = ['+', '-', '*', '/'];
```

You now need to generate a list of numbers that are selected using the big and small counts:

```
const numbers = [];
for (let i = 0; i < bigCount; i++) {
  const index = Math.floor(
    Math.random() * bigNumbers.length
  );
  numbers.push(bigNumbers[index]);
}
for (let i = 0; i < smallCount; i++) {
  const index = Math.floor(
    Math.random() * smallNumbers.length
  );
  numbers.push(smallNumbers[index]);
}
```

This gives you the numbers that need to be used to calculate the target. You can see the use of `Math.random()` to select a random index in the big and small numbers arrays, and then the selected number is pushed into the `numbers` array.

About the target... There are times on the Numbers Game when the answer can't be solved – it's rare but it happens. This is not the experience you want for the players, so you need to be sure the games can be solved. The means you can use a little magic-behind-the-scenes (a.k.a cheating) to ensure it can be done. Instead of generating a random number for the target you generate a random equation and the result *becomes* the target.

But first you need a shuffle function. Why? Because at some point in the game you'll need to show the answer, and if the answer looks suspicious or predictable then people might complain. You need to shuffle the numbers so it looks like you worked hard on the answer.

```
const shuffle = (array) => {
  const copied = [...array];
  const shuffled = [];
```

```
while (copied.length > 0) {
  const index = Math.floor(
    Math.random() * copied.length
  );
  shuffled.push(copied[index]);
  copied.splice(index, 1);
}
return shuffled;
};
```

The **shuffle** function makes a copy of the **array** argument. This is because the **splice** method will modify the original array. In some situations this is fine, but in this case you don't want to change the original because you need to show those numbers later:

```
const generate = (numbers) => {
  return {
    numbers
  };
};

const result = generate(numbers);
console.log(result);
```

Before you return the **numbers** you need to create a shuffled version of it, so now you can add the **shuffle** result:

```
const shuffled = shuffle(numbers);
```

Feel free to add that to the returned object so you can see what's happening:

```
return {
  numbers: numbers.join(', '),
  shuffled: shuffled.join(', ')
};
```

And now to create the equation that calculates the target number. Let's break down what needs to happen:

- Ensure the target is between 101 and 999
- For every number, apply an operator (+, -, x, /) to the current target and the number
- Ensure that if the divide operator (/) is used it won't create decimals
- When it's complete it should output the target, the numbers used and the answer.

You can start by declaring the current total and the workings:

```
let currentTotal = 0;
let workings = '';
```

When dealing with random values it's difficult to know when (or if) the results will be ready. There's also the issue of division: if you divide a number and it creates a decimal then it will prevent the result from being a whole number.

You know that the target must be between 101 and 999 for it to be valid, and it should keep working until it finds a valid result, so:

```
while (currentTotal < 101 || currentTotal > 999) {
```

The condition in this **while** loop will ensure the code it executes will continue to iterate until it's been met – a target between 101 and 999.

```
currentTotal = shuffled[0];
workings = `${currentTotal}`;

for (let i = 1; i < shuffled.length; i++) {
  const operatorIndex = Math.floor(
    Math.random() * operators.length
  );
  const operator = operators[operatorIndex];
  const number = shuffled[i];
```

By setting the **currentTotal** and **workings** to the first number gives you something to start with. It also means the **for** loop should start at 1.

About the division issue. If the current **operator** is / you need to check that it's not going to create any decimals (or remainders) when it's used. If it does then you need to stop the **for** loop and start again.

```
if (operator === '/' && currentTotal % number !== 0) {
    currentTotal = 0;
    break;
}
```

- 6 / 3 = 2 – good
- 5 / 2 = 2.5 – bad
- 1 / 3 = 0.33333 – very bad

That condition will **break** the **for** loop and reset the **currentTotal**. This will cause the **while** loop to begin the process again. But if the values are good then you can continue to build:

```
switch (operator) {
    case '+':
        currentTotal += number;
        break;
    case '-':
        currentTotal -= number;
        break;
    case '*':
        currentTotal *= number;
        break;
    case '/':
        currentTotal /= number;
        break;
}

workings += ` ${operator} ${number}`;
```

Different things happen between the **currentTotal** and the **number** depending on the **operator**. As the **currentTotal** is updated you also need to update the **workings**. Sting concatenation is fine, but if you prefer you could have used an array and pushed the operator and number into it.

Here's the whole **generate** function:

```
const generate = (numbers) => {
```

```javascript
const shuffled = shuffle(numbers);

let currentTotal = 0;
let workings = '';
while (currentTotal < 101 || currentTotal > 999) {
  currentTotal = shuffled[0];
  workings = `${currentTotal}`;

  for (let i = 1; i < shuffled.length; i++) {
    const operatorIndex = Math.floor(
      Math.random() * operators.length
    );
    const operator = operators[operatorIndex];
    const number = shuffled[i];

    if (operator === '/' &&
        currentTotal % number !== 0) {
      currentTotal = 0;
      break;
    }

    switch (operator) {
      case '+':
        currentTotal += number;
        break;
      case '-':
        currentTotal -= number;
        break;
      case '*':
        currentTotal *= number;
        break;
      case '/':
        currentTotal /= number;
        break;
    }

    workings += ` ${operator} ${number}`;
```

```
    }
  }

  return {
    numbers: numbers.join(', '),
    currentTotal,
    workings
  };
};
```

The returned **numbers** have been joined so they more readable (but you don't have to do that if you have other plans). This is one potential result of the **generate** function (1 large, 5 small):

```
{
  currentTotal: 144,
  numbers: '75, 7, 3, 6, 2, 9',
  workings: '2 * 3 + 7 * 6 - 9 + 75'
}
```

You can check the workings by calculating left-to-right (ignore rules about BODMAS or PEDMAS):

- $2 * 3 + 7 * 6 - 9 + 75$
- $6 + 7 * 6 - 9 + 75$
- $13 * 6 - 9 + 75$
- $78 - 9 + 75$
- $69 + 75$
- 144

Now let's try 2 large and 5 small:

```
{
  currentTotal: 574,
  numbers: '25, 75, 7, 8, 9, 6',
  workings: '9 + 8 + 25 / 6 + 75 * 7'
}
```

That works too! Congratulations on re-creating the Numbers Game.

Validating the Numbers Game

When working with random numbers, multiple loops and potentially unknown inputs the chance for errors or incorrect results becomes substantially high, and while it's great to think the code you write is *perfect*, it can be a better idea to prove it. Better again if you have a fallback that can fix the problem if/when it happens.

Take the previous result:

```
{
  currentTotal: 574,
  numbers: '25, 75, 7, 8, 9, 6',
  workings: '9 + 8 + 25 / 6 + 75 * 7'
}
```

There are some checks that can be performed on that – if they're all clear then that's great. Otherwise it would be better to regenerate the result until it's perfect.

- Check that the right number of numbers were selected
- Check that all the numbers are used in the working
- Check that the workings result in the target

You can start by creating a new validation function. For this you just want to know if the result is correct, so returning a Boolean value is all that's needed. If any of the checks fail then it needs to **return false** right away.

```
const validate = (result) => {
  const target = result.currentTotal;
  const nums = result.numbers.split(', ');
  const workings = result.workings.split(' ');
```

Using **split** helps to separate the values to make them easier to process. With **numb** being a comma-separated list it's safe to use the comma/space combo, but if you didn't join them earlier then this part isn't necessary – you could instead just get the **nums** array:

```
const { numbers: nums } = result;
```

If you created this validation script in the same file as the **generate** script then you might have noticed the sudden change of **numbers** to **nums**. You had declared a high-level **numbers** array earlier, so any attempt to redeclare it will give you an error. That's why the variable name had to change (also when destructuring you can rename the variable to be something else).

Now check that the **nums** array has the correct number of values:

```
if (numb.length !== bigCount + smallCount) {
  console.log('wrong number of numbers');
  return false;
}
```

It would be easy to write the 6 in there, but as long as you can rely on the big and small numbers being correct then it's better to use them to ensure the number is also correct. The **console.log** is more for your initial benefit so that if there was a problem you could quickly find it. The **return false** makes the **validate** function immediately return the value.

The next test is to ensure the same numbers are in the workings. Unfortunately the **workings** is a string, and even though it was **split** each item is a string and nearly half of them are operators. The actual valid numbers need to be filtered out:

```
const validNumbers = nums.filter((number) => {
  return parseInt(number, 10);
});
```

Now you can check if the **numbers** and **validNumbers** are the same:

```
if (validNumbers !== nums) {
  console.log('invalid numbers', validNumbers, nums);
  return false;
}
```

Hold on, do you remember that **shuffle** function from before? The one you used to make sure the workings didn't look like you randomly placed operators between the numbers? Arrays don't get compared the same way as strings and numbers. Even if they have the same values but the order is incorrect then they won't be seen as the same. They need a little more work:

```
if (validNumbers.sort().join(',') !==
  nums.sort().join(',')) {
  console.log('invalid numbers', validNumbers, nums);
  return false;
}
```

Both of them need to be sorted and then joined. Why? Check this out:

```
const a = [1, 2, 3];
const b = [1, 2, 3];

console.log(a === a); // true
console.log(a === b); // false
```

Here both **a** and **b** have the exact same items in the same order (like what happens after sorting). If you compare **a** against itself then it returns **true**, but when you try it with **b** it returns **false**. The reason is because arrays are *technically* objects in JavaScript.

```
console.log(typeof a); // 'object'
```

When comparing objects they don't use the values. Instead they're checked to see if they're reference is the same: it's how they're stored in memory.

```
const a = [1, 2, 3];
const b = [1, 2, 3];
const c = a;

console.log(a === a); // true
console.log(a === b); // false
console.log(a === c); // true
```

Here **a** and **c** share the same reference, so JavaScript says they're the same. Therefore, sorting and joining is necessary. How they're sorted isn't important either as long as it's the same kind of sorting.

It should be noted sorting and joining the arrays is specific to this situation. Converting an array to a string has its drawback, in particular if the array contains objects instead of numbers and strings. There are other ways to check for equality, but they all depend on what you plan to test them with.

Back to the validation: it's a good idea to check that the first value in the **workings** array is a number – you're going to need it very soon:

```
if (!parseInt(workings[0])) {
  console.log('first item is not a number');
  return false;
}
```

The next step is to 'manually' calculate the target using the **workings**. It's very similar to the code you wrote to generate the target earlier except for the fact that the **operator** is not on its own. Using a **forEach** method on the **workings** is correct, but different things need to happen depending on the current item:

- If it's the first item then the current total needs to be set
- If the item is an operator, then it needs to be stored because...
- If the item is a number it needs to use the operator on the current total

```
let currentTotal = 0;
let operator = '';
workings.forEach((item, i) => {
  if (i === 0) {
    currentTotal = parseInt(item);
```

```
  } else if (i % 2 !== 0) {
    operator = item;
  } else {
    switch(operator) {
      case '+':
        currentTotal += parseInt(item);
        break;
      case '-':
        currentTotal -= parseInt(item);
        break;
      case '*':
        currentTotal *= parseInt(item);
        break;
      case '/':
        currentTotal /= parseInt(item);
        break;
    }
  }
});
```

This aims to replicate the same approach you used to check that the **workings** were correct. Working left-to-right and applying the operators and numbers together to calculate the target.

Now that you have it, check it:

```
if (currentTotal !== target) {
  console.log('invalid total', currentTotal, target);
  return false;
}

return true;
```

Like other tests if it isn't valid it should **return false**. But that's the last test, so make sure to finish it with **return true**.

You've now written a validation script. Here's the full version:

```
const validate = (result) => {
  const target = result.currentTotal;
```

```javascript
const { numbers } = result;
const nums = result.numbers.split(', ');
const workings = result.workings.split(' ');

if (nums.length !== bigCount + smallCount) {
  console.log('wrong number of numbers');
  return false;
}

const validNumbers = nums.filter((number) => {
  return parseInt(number, 10);
});

if (validNumbers.sort().join(',') !== nums.sort().join(',')) {
  console.log('invalid numbers', validNumbers, numbers);
  return false;
}

if (!parseInt(workings[0])) {
  console.log('first item is not a number');
  return false;
}

let currentTotal = 0;
let operator = '';
workings.forEach((item, i) => {
  if (i === 0) {
    currentTotal = parseInt(item);
  } else if (i % 2 !== 0) {
    operator = item;
  } else {
    switch(operator) {
      case '+':
        currentTotal += parseInt(item);
        break;
      case '-':
        currentTotal -= parseInt(item);
```

```
        break;
      case '*':
        currentTotal *= parseInt(item);
        break;
      case '/':
        currentTotal /= parseInt(item);
        break;
    }
  }
});

if (currentTotal !== target) {
  console.log('invalid total', currentTotal, target);
  return false;
}

return true;
};

console.log(validate(result));
```

There are a variety of testing tools in the wild that you can use to verify that your code works under real-world conditions. As of 2024 there's Jest, Mocha, Jasmine, Cypress and Enzyme along with others that allow you to write and test your code and functions at the same time. Using them is often preferred to writing your own framework, but you need to write the actual tests: they help to automate the testing process to help improve your confidence in the code (and alert you if tests fail).

Basic sentiment analysis

A film review site has recently added the ability to pick emojis when writing reviews. During testing people liked the choices but didn't like the order they were shown. They said that if the comment was good then the 'positive' emojis should be shown first, and if the comment was bad then the 'negative' emojis should be first instead.

You might think that an advanced form of sentiment analysis would be useful here, possibly involving machine learning, but then you find out you don't have long to work on this so it needs to be a quick solution:

- Find keywords in the comment to indicate
- Score the comment based on the keywords
- Order the emojis based on the score

To start, you need to know which words to search for:

```
const model = {
  positive: ['loved', 'liked', 'awesome', 'amazing', 'good',
'great', 'excellent', 'fantastic'],
  negative: ['hated', 'disliked', 'awful', 'terrible', 'bad',
'poor', 'sucks', 'disappointing'],
};
```

This **model** can have words added over time, and it doesn't have to take into account the context, sarcasm or other nuances of language – it's a quick and dirty solution. Next is the emojis:

```
const emojis = {
  positive: ['😀', '😊', '👍', '😄'],
  neutral: ['😶', '😑', '😐', '😕'],
  negative: ['😞', '😨', '👎', '😠'],
};
```

You might have noticed that there are no **neutral** words in the **model**, but there are **neutral** emojis. That's because a comment could be neutral overall, for example: 'I liked the film, but the seats were terrible'.

This is how you could determine the sentiment:

```
const sentiment = (text) => {
  let score = 0;
  const words = text.toLowerCase().split(/\W/);
  words.forEach((word) => {
    if (model.positive.includes(word)) {
      score++;
    } else if (model.negative.includes(word)) {
      score--;
    }
  });

  // ...
};
```

The **text** is converted to lowercase and splits it on all non-word characters (the **\W** regex token) to get the individual **words**. Then each **word** is compared to the values in the **positive** and **negative** arrays — if the **word** is there then the **score** is increased or decreased depending on which array has includes the **word**.

As for the order? Don't worry about sorting them. Instead you can return an array with a more specific order using the spread operator:

```
if (score > 0) {
  // if score is positive
  return [
    ...emojis.positive,
```

```
      ...emojis.neutral,
      ...emojis.negative
    ];
  } else if (score < 0) {
    // if score is negative
    return [
      ...emojis.negative,
      ...emojis.neutral,
      ...emojis.positive
    ];
  }
  // score is neutral
  return [
    ...emojis.neutral,
    ...emojis.positive,
    ...emojis.negative
  ];
```

This gives you more control over which group of emojis are shown first. You could also modify it to show more options if the score exceeds a threshold. If the score if over 10 then you could add various emojis like ⭐ , ✅ and 🥂 , but too negative and you can give users 💩 , 💥 and 🗑 as some options.

Recommendations

You've been asked to create a recommendation system for Solstice Isle Airlines. The customers all start from Solstice and travel to different parts of the continent. To help create this system you're given some historical data:

```
const history = {
  Bob: ['Solstice Isle', 'Veridia', 'Etherinia City', 'Solstice
Isle'],
  Alice: ['Solstice Isle', 'Veridia', 'Etherinia City', 'Solstice
Isle'],
  Jane: ['Solstice Isle', 'Veridia', 'Etherinia City', 'Solstice
Isle'],
  Carol: ['Solstice Isle', 'Veridia', 'Solstice Isle'],
  Ted: ['Solstice Isle', 'Etherinia City']
};
```

Already you can see that the three most common routes depart from Solstice Isle, make their way to Veridia, stop over at Etherinia City then return home. Using that knowledge you can recommend the most popular route:

```
const routes = Object.values(history);
const counts = routes.reduce((accumulator, route) => {
  if (!accumulator[route]) {
    accumulator[route] = 0;
```

```
    }
    accumulator[route] += 1;

    return accumulator;
}, {});
```

Which produced this object:

```
{
    'Solstice Isle,Veridia,Etherinia City,Solstice Isle': 3,
    'Solstice Isle,Veridia,Solstice Isle': 1,
    'Solstice Isle,Etherinia City': 1
}
```

And to get the route:

```
const mostFrequent = Object.entries(counts).sort((a, b) => b[1] -
a[1])[0];
```

This code will get the job done (even if it is messy) and it will give you the most frequent flight. While that might be useful it's not taking into account other destinations.

While selecting destinations it would be great if the option was pre-selected if the customer's previous destinations matched the historical ones. You can rewrite the previous code to generate a model:

```
const model = Object.values(history).reduce((accumulator, routes)
=> {
    const id = routes.join('->');
    if (!accumulator[id]) {
        accumulator[id] = {
            routes,
            count: 0,
        };
    }
    accumulator[id].count += 1;

    return accumulator;
}, {});
```

This gives you the ability to find possible routes, sort them to get the most frequent, and then return the next possible destination. Let's say Abby (new customer) will depart Solstice Isle and has selected Veridia as their next destination. The model lets you search for previous routes like this:

```
const predictNextRoute = (routes) => {
  const id = routes.join('->');

  // Find routes that contain the current route in their key
  const possibleRoutes = Object.keys(model).filter((route) =>
    route.includes(id)
  );

  return possibleRoutes;
};

predictNextRoute(['Solstice Isle', 'Veridia']);
```

You now have the keys for the model object to get the next possible option/s. This can be extended further to get the most frequent route and return with the next option:

```
const predictNextRoute = (routes) => {
  const id = routes.join("->");

  // Find routes that contain the current route in their key
  const possibleRoutes = Object.keys(model)
    .filter((route) => route.includes(id))
    .map((route) => model[route]);

  // Sort by count and get the first one
  const mostFrequent = possibleRoutes.sort((a, b) => b.count -
a.count);

  // Get the last route in the customer's selected routes
  const lastCustomerRoute = routes[routes.length - 1];
```

```
// If there are no routes or the last route is not in the most
frequent route, return null
if (mostFrequent.length === 0 || !mostFrequent) {
  return null;
}

// Get the most frequent route
const bestRoute = mostFrequent[0];

// Get the next route in the most frequent route
const next = bestRoute.routes.indexOf(lastCustomerRoute) + 1;
if (bestRoute.routes[next]) {
  return bestRoute.routes[next];
}

// If there is no next route, return null
return null;
};
```

Let's break this down:

- just like earlier it gets the keys of all routes that match the fragment of what the customer has selected
- it sorts the returned routes to get the most frequent
- performs a quick check to make sure the function should continue
- using the customer's last known destination, gets the index of the next one from the most frequent route
- returns the destination using the key
- returns **null** otherwise

When the customer chooses their second destination, you can run this to find another to recommend:

```
predictNextRoute(['Solstice Isle', 'Veridia']);
```

...which will return Etherinia City. And if/when they choose that:

```
predictNextRoute(['Solstice Isle', 'Veridia', 'Etherinia City']);
```

...they complete the round trip and arrive back at Solstice Isle.

The strings used for this project help to demonstrate the data, but it would be better if those were replaced with ids.

```
const destinations = {
  sol: {
    name: 'Solstice Isle',
  },
  ver: {
    name: 'Veridia',
  },
  eth: {
    name: 'Etherinia',
  },
  lat: {
    name: 'Latania Cove',
  }
};
```

And then this:

```
predictNextRoute(['sol', 'ver', 'eth']);
```

This would enable you to reduce the amount of text used in the strings. It also means you can update the UI with information about flights, for example:

- SOL-314 to Veridia departing at 9:00am

Undo/redo

While working on a single page application you've been asked to include a new feature: the ability to undo (and redo) the changes your client will make.

Arrays are great for this – every time an action is made you can push the previous state into an array. When the time comes to undo the action, you just need to get the most recent value from the array and change the state.

Let's take some basic data:

```
const data = { hello: 'world' };
```

You know this **data** needs to be updated when changes are made while also managing the history, so a class would be useful:

```
class UndoRedo {
  constructor(data) {
    this.data = data;
    this.undoStack = [];
    this.redoStack = [];
  }

  set(props) {}
  undo() {}
  redo() {}
}
```

The **constructor** has three parts: a *reference* to your **data** variable (not the data itself) and two stacks, one each for undo and redo actions. You should now initialise the class:

```
const proxy = new UndoRedo(data);
```

You've passed in the **data** variable as the argument. When it's time to make a change you need to use the **proxy**:

```
proxy.set({ yolo: 'swag' });
```

As for the **set** method:

```
set(props) {
  this.undoStack.push({ ...this.data });
  this.redoStack = [];
  Object.assign(this.data, props);
}
```

First it pushes the current value of your data into the **undoStack** array and then clears the **redoStack** array. Clearing the redo stack after a new action is an expected thing, so you should continue that. The new **props** are then assigned to the **data** reference.

The **Object.assign** method will merge the new **props** with the existing ones in **this.data**:

```
console.log(data); // { hello: 'world', yolo: 'swag' }
```

As you can see the original **data** and the new **props** are now together. To undo that change:

```
undo() {
  if (this.undoStack.length === 0) {
    console.log('No actions to undo');
    return;
  }

  this.redoStack.push({ ...this.data });
  const state = this.undoStack.pop();
```

```
  Object.keys(this.data).forEach(
    (key) => delete this.data[key]
  );
  Object.assign(this.data, state);
}
```

You should always check to see if there's anything in the stack to **undo**. If there is you should **push** the current **data** value into the **redoStack** before getting the most recent value from the **undoStack** and assigning it to the **data**.

Because **Object.assign** merges object data you need to clear it otherwise the **data** won't be correct. It's nearly the same for **redo**: you just need to swap the arrays:

```
redo() {
  if (this.redoStack.length === 0) {
    console.log('No actions to redo');
    return;
  }

  this.undoStack.push({ ...this.data });
  const state = this.redoStack.pop();
  Object.keys(this.data).forEach(
    (key) => delete this.data[key]
  );
  Object.assign(this.data, state);
}
```

How about a quick test to make sure it works:

```
proxy.set({ more: [1, 2, 3] });
console.log(data);
// { hello: 'world', yolo: 'swag', more: [1, 2, 3] }

proxy.undo();
console.log(data);
// { hello: 'world', yolo: 'swag' }
```

And then **redo**:

```
proxy.redo();
console.log(data);
// { hello: 'world', yolo: 'swag', more: [1, 2, 3] }
```

It's a basic class but it works! If you update the **data** without using the **proxy** then the undo and redo stacks will become out of sync. If that's a necessary workflow in your app then you can add some more methods to your class:

```
clear() {
  this.undoStack = [];
  this.redoStack = [];
}

reset(data) {
  this.clear();
  this.data = data;
}
```

The **clear** method empties both stacks and **reset** will reset the reference to your **data**. This enables you to continue to use the undo/redo feature if the data changes (like after saving the data to an API and getting a new object returned).

Browser fingerprinting

Browser fingerprinting uses a combination of values provided by the user's browser, such as their language, time zone and screen size. Individually they have no impact, but when combined they can act as a unique identifier. Some people use them for tracking users across websites, others use it for security: you've been asked to help with the latter:

To give the fingerprint enough 'uniqueness' you need to get the:

- user agent
- language
- width, height and supported colours of the screen
- time zone and locale
- supported plugins, and
- supported fonts

These values are used because they don't change frequently (and they're also available when using private browsing). You can start with first few – they're the easy ones:

```
const { userAgent, language } = window.navigator;
const { width, height, colorDepth } = window.screen;
```

And now you can add those values to an object:

```
const fingerprint = {
  userAgent,
```

```
    language,
    width,
    height,
    colorDepth
};
```

As more is added to the **fingerprint** object you'll need to find a way to reduce its complexity while keeping its uniqueness. That's where Hashing comes in: it's a mathematical transformation where the original value becomes something else and once it's changed it can't be reverted back (which is different from encryption and decryption). You're going to use a variation of the DJB2[5] hashing algorithm:

```
const jsonToString = JSON.stringify(fingerprint);
```

That converts the object into a string which is necessary for the actual hashing:

```
let hash = 0;
jsonToString.split('').forEach((char) => {
  hash = (hash << 5) + hash + char.charCodeAt(0);
});

console.log(fingerprint, hash);
```

The string is **split** and for each character it undergoes a bitwise operation (the **<<**). Here's how it works for the first eight letters of the alphabet:

Letter	Calculation	Hash
a	(0 << 5) + 0 + 97	97
b	(97 << 5) + 97 + 98	3299
c	(3299 << 5) + 3299 + 99	108966
d	(108966 << 5) + 108966 + 100	3595978
e	(3595978 << 5) + 3595978 + 101	118667475
f	(118667475 << 5) + 118667475 + 102	-378943819
g	(-378943819 << 5) + -378943819 + 103	379755964

---

[5] http://www.cse.yorku.ca/~oz/hash.html

150

If you've never seen a bitwise operation before then here's what it does: it converts the number into binary and then (in this case) shifts the value five 0s to the left before converting it back to a decimal, like this:

```
1 = 0000 0001
1 << 5 = 0010 0000 = 32
```

The limitations of the bitwise operator are where it becomes destructive (and a little technical): the 32nd bit of a binary number determines if it's positive or negative. For the first six letters of the alphabet there are 30 bit-shifts, so when it does letter 'g' the shift flips the 32nd bit to a negative. You can test it like this:

```
let current = 1;
let count = 1;
while (current > 0) {
  console.log(current, count);
  current = current << 1;
  count++;
}
console.log(current, count);
```

It also has the benefit of capping the value to prevent it from growing, so now as more hashing occurs the overall length of the **hash** won't change. Speaking of growing, it's time to add the time zone and locale:

```
const { timeZone: timezone, locale } =
Intl.DateTimeFormat().resolvedOptions();
```

The **resolvedOptions** has a **timeZone** property which you can rename to **timezone**. You can add them to the **fingerprint**:

```
const fingerprint = {
  ...
  colorDepth,
  timezone, // <- new
  locale // <- also new
```

If you check the value of the **fingerprint** you might notice that **language** and **locale** are different (depends on where you are). The **language** is specific to the language the operating system is set to, while the **locale** is specific to the user's location and time zone. There's no guarantee they will be the same.

Plugins aren't as prolific as they used to be – Adobe Flash, Shockwave, RealPlayer – but they can still be used in the fingerprint (again, not something that changes often):

```
const plugins = Array.from(window.navigator.plugins).map(
  (plugin) => plugin.name
);
```

And like **timezone** and **locale** it can also be added to the **fingerprint**. The last piece involves fonts, and these are not easy. Browsers don't give this information up freely so you need to be a little creative. You can confirm that a font is supported by checking to see if it's drawn.

Let's say you have a short list of fonts you wanted to check (you can add more later):

```
const testFonts = [
  '67ve567b457e456',
  'Arial',
  'Arial Black',
  'Comic Sans MS',
  'Courier New',
  'Georgia',
  'Impact',
  'Lucida Console',
  'Lucida Sans Unicode',
  'Palatino Linotype',
  'Tahoma',
  'Times New Roman',
  'Trebuchet MS',
  'Verdana'
];
```

The first one isn't a typo – it's highly unlikely you'd have a font by that name, so it's a good way to test what you're about to write works – that font won't be supported.

If a browser is asked to render text in a font it doesn't have it will render it in another. If you know the size of that text when using the default font, you can compare it against the supported font because it will be a different size.

This is where the `canvas` element comes in. Typically, you would use a `canvas` to draw things, but for now you're going to use it to measure the text.

```
const fonts = [];
const canvas = document.createElement('canvas');
const ctx = canvas.getContext('2d');
const text = 'abcdefghijklmnopqrstuvwxyz0123456789';
ctx.font = '72px monospace';
const baselineSize = ctx.measureText(text).width;
```

The `fonts` array will store the supported fonts (and go into the `fingerprint` later). It then creates a `canvas` element and gets the `ctx`, or context, which will be used for all drawing purposes. By setting the `ctx.font` to `72px monospace` allows you to measure the `width` of the text using the `ctx.measureText` method. If any font you're about to test has another width, then it confirms that it's a supported font.

```
testFonts.forEach((font) => {
  ctx.font = `72px ${font}, monospace`;
  const size = ctx.measureText(text).width;
  if (size !== baselineSize) {
    fonts.push(font);
  }
});
```

It sets the font property again, except it combines the font you want to test with the monospace font from earlier: if the `font` isn't supported it will use the monospace font instead. If the measured `size` is not the same as the `baselineSize`, then the `font` is supported and can be added to the `fonts` array.

Your fingerprint should now look like this:

```
const fingerprint = {
  userAgent,
  language,
  width,
  height,
  colorDepth,
  timezone,
  locale,
  plugins,
  fonts
};
```

You can make one last change:

```
console.log(fingerprint, hash.toString(16));
```

By changing the **hash** number into a hexadecimal string (**toString(16)**) you get a result that looks a little more technical and takes up fewer characters.

And that's it – you've successfully fingerprinted a browser.

Hidden text message

Your client is angry. It started when they learned that bots were scaping their website for content and republishing it on other sites. Now they've found that large language models (LLMs) were trained using their website and their hard work is now being used to show how great AI is. They've become hesitant to post their next set of articles knowing they'll have to contend with a number of bots and systems that are ready to rip them off.

They've asked you to try and find a solution. You've already done some work with machine learning and you know how important it is for these models to have accurate training data in order to give a decent result.

Fortunately, this is an issue that's been dealt with before: it's called a copyright trap. Once upon a time map publishers added fake landmarks that had no impact on people navigating, but if it showed up in a competitor's map then they knew they'd been copied. Dictionaries, encyclopedias and other reference texts also added false entries that would indicate the theft of content. So how can you add similar artifacts to text on a website to indicate it had been copied without adding a bunch of false information?

What if you could add a trap to the text by changing the characters? You would need to:

- Reduce the complexity of the message to make it easier to hide
- Find a way to hide the message in plain sight
- Create a way to find out if the message is in the content

Before high-speed internet, dial-up internet, fax and phones there was Morse code: a series of dots and dashes that could be used to transmit text.

This is what it looks like:

- 'Hello' becomes '.... . .-.. .-.. ---'

Converting your message into Morse code would help to simplify the embedded result. This is the full map of Morse code:

```
const morseCode = {
  a: '.-', b: '-...', c: '-.-.', d: '-..',
  e: '.', f: '..-.', g: '--.', h: '....',
  i: '..', j: '.---', k: '-.-', l: '.-..',
  m: '--', n: '-.', o: '---', p: '.--.',
  q: '--.-', r: '.-.', s: '...', t: '-',
  u: '..-', v: '...-', w: '.--', x: '-..-',
  y: '-.--', z: '--..', 0: '-----', 1: '.----',
  2: '..---', 3: '...--', 4: '....-', 5: '.....',
  6: '-....', 7: '--...', 8: '---..', 9: '----.',
  '.': '.-.-.-', ',': '--..--'
};
```

And to convert your message into these dots and dashes:

```
const morse = (str) =>
  str
    .toLowerCase()
    .replace(/[^a-z0-9., ]/g, '')
    .split('')
    .map((el) => morseCode[el] || '')
    .join('/');
```

This function takes your message string, makes it all lowercase, removes unnecessary characters and replaces the remaining ones with their Morse code equivalent. All spaces are replaced by forward-slashes.

This greatly reduces the range of characters you need to hide – from 26 letters, 10 numbers and some punctuation down to three – dot, dash and a separator. But you still need them to appear normal when you embed them in the text. And that's where Unicode comes in. There are numerous Unicode characters that *look* the same but have different values behind the scenes. If you find some Unicode characters that look the same as normal characters in the text you can assign them their new value to represent each dot and dash.

Take this length of content:

- Once upon a moonlit lagoon, a colossal, monolithic monsoon of opulent obsidian orbs overflowed, orchestrating an ostentatious opera of oscillating octagons.

That's a lot of 'o'. Which is perfect because there are three Unicode characters that *look* like an 'o', but really aren't:

```
const map = {
  '.': '\u043e', // Cyrillic small letter O
  '-': '\u03bf', // Greek small letter for Omicron
  '/': '\u0585' // Armenian comma
};
```

By assigning these characters to their Morse code values you can replace the values in the text with their new characters:

```
const embedMessage = (str, message) => {
  const code = morse(`${message} `).split('');
```

The **embedMessage** function accepts two arguments: the string you want the message to be embedded into, and the **message** itself. With that done, you can convert the message into Morse code. Yes, there is an extra space added to the end of the message: the message needs to loop through the text, so adding a space will help later with knowing when the last character ends and the first begins.

Now for the rest:

```
  let counter = 0;
  return str.replace(/[o]/gm, () => {
    const char = code[counter % code.length];
    counter++;
    return map[char];
  });
};
```

For every 'o' in the string it needs to be replaced by the Unicode character. The index used for the `char` (`code[counter % code.length]`) allows it to continue to loop regardless of the length of the string.

Let's see what happens:

```
const story = `Once upon a moonlit lagoon, a colossal, monolithic
monsoon of opulent obsidian orbs overflowed orchestrating an
ostentatious opera.`;

const converted = embedMessage(story, 'Copyright, 2024');
console.log(converted);
```

The output should *look* the same as the original message. But every 'o' has been replaced with a Unicode character that represents either a dot, dash or a separator.

Now that you've added the **message** it's time to create a way to recover it:

```
const recoverMessage = (str) => {
  const pattern = new RegExp(`[${Object.values(map).join('')}]+`,
'gm');
```

The **recoverMessage** function uses a regular expression with the values of the **map** from before. This is necessary because you need to get all the Unicode characters to read the **message**:

```
  const chars = str.match(pattern).join('').split('');
```

In the original text 'orbs' has a single 'o' but 'moonlit' has two. In that case the result of the **match** method will return both results ('o' and 'oo'), but you need them to be separate as each of them will be converted to their Morse code equivalent:

```
  const code = chars
    .map((quote) => Object.keys(map).find(
      (key) => map[key] === quote)
    )
    .join('')
    .split('/');
```

This Morse code array now needs to be converted back to English:

```
const message = code
  .map((el) => Object.keys(morseCode).find(
    (key) => morseCode[key] === el)
  )
  .join('');

  return message;
};
```

This is the reverse of the letter to Morse code conversion – it's looking for the key based on the matching value. Time to check to see if the recovery works:

```
const unconverted = recoverMessage(converted);
console.log(unconverted);
```

And the result:

- copyr

The rest of the message isn't there because of the small amount of text in the original content, but if there is enough text then it will appear in full.

There are some downsides to this – you're adding letters that might be unreadable by screen-readers and other assistive technologies. Fortunately, it's easy enough to use spaces instead. There a plenty of whitespace characters to choose from, but here's some options:

```
const map = {
  '.': '\u2000', // En quad
  '-': '\u2002', // En space
  '/': '\u2004' // Three-per-em space
};
```

And don't forget to update the **embedMessage**:

```
return str.replace(/[ ]/gm, () => {
```

Because of the work you did earlier these changes are all you need. When you test it you might notice that the recovered message isn't exactly the same (it might be a little short). That's because there are fewer spaces than 'o' characters in the text content.

You could also be a little more devious in your embedded message. You could embed the original author's name, the date, or if your client's site requires a login to see the content you could embed part of the user's email (as long as it doesn't violate laws surrounding personal information).

While it's possible to detect Unicode characters you need to be looking for them first. And if different replacements are used on different days (not just 'o' and whitespace characters) it makes detection even more difficult.

Advanced projects

You're ready for the advanced stuff? Of course you are! Time to dive into the deep-end, and with everything you've learned so far you'll be able to take these projects and *bend* them to your will.

These projects are more complex and require you to think a little more outside the box. They're all do-able, but some concepts might challenge you a more than others. If that's the case just continue with it, and once you get a result try going back and changing the way it works to see what happens. That's the joy of working with any coding language: you can always change it.

Custom web components

Your client's aging site needs a serious update, but both time and money are limited. Updating the site to use a reactive framework like React, Vue, Svelte or Angular is not an option but changes are *desperately* needed: the product prices and delivery times need a refactor as they're always incorrectly formatted. Web components might be the option you're looking for.

Web components have a lot in common with the components used by React, Vue and Svelte except they're completely native to JavaScript (no extra runtime or compiler needed). They look like this:

```
class CustomComponent extends HTMLElement {
  constructor() {
    super();
  }

  connectedCallback() {
    this.render();
  }

  render() {
    this.textContent = 'Hello, world!';
  }
}
```

```
customElements.define('custom-component', CustomComponent, {
  extends: 'div'
});
```

You can see it starts like other classes where it starts with a **constructor**. When the component successfully connects to the HTML page (or DOM) the **render** function is then run. The **customElements** is reserved for web components and is used to **define** how the element will be used in the HTML. So for a component that formats a currency to be correct for the user:

```
class CurrencyFormatter extends HTMLSpanElement {
  constructor() {
    super();
  }

  connectedCallback() {
    this.render();
  }

  render() {
    const amount = this.getAttribute('amount');
    const currency = this.getAttribute('currency');

    const formatter = new Intl.NumberFormat(undefined, {
      style: 'currency',
      currencyDisplay: 'narrowSymbol',
      currency
    });
    this.textContent = formatter.format(amount);
  }
}
```

It all happens in the **render**:

1. the **currency** attribute is used with the **Intl.NumberFormat** to create a **formatter**
2. the formatter is used on the **amount** attribute when setting the element's **textContent**

For this example, the component will be used as an inline element so the **extends HTMLSpanElement** is used, but you could use a block-level element like a paragraph if you want.

If you refreshed your browser page you'd see nothing because it's not expecting any components, so now's the time to define it:

```
customElements.define('currency-formatter', CurrencyFormatter, {
  extends: 'span',
});
```

And this is how you'd use it in your HTML page:

```
<p>
  You paid
  <currency-formatter currency="AUD" amount="100.5"></currency-
formatter>
  for that item.
</p>
```

Now you should see this in your browser:

- You paid $100.50 for that item.

In the **Intl.NumberFormat** there was no locale defined, so the browser will use the user's locale. The currency in the component is set to AUD (Australian Dollars).

This won't handle the conversion of the currency itself – just the way it's shown. If the browser doesn't recognise the currency it will show the value at the front (replacing any symbol):

```
<currency-formatter currenry="XBT" amount="100.5"></currency-
formatter>
```

- You paid XBT 100.50 for that item.

What about time? You could have a component to show when the purchase was made or when the expected delivery will be. Start with the component first:

```
<p><time-formatter datetime="2024-03-07T04:30:00Z"></time-
formatter></p>
```

The **datetime** attribute will be used by the component to display a more human-readable value. Now for the definition:

```
class TimeFormatter extends HTMLTimeElement {
```

Using **HTMLTimeElement** instead of **HTMLSpanElement** is a minor change but will help with assistive technologies. Now jump to the **render** method:

```
render() {
  const datetime = this.getAttribute('datetime');
  const date = new Date(datetime);
  const formatter = new Intl.RelativeTimeFormat(undefined, {
    style: 'long'
  });
```

Similar to before you're getting the **datetime** attribute and then converting it into a real **Date**. And you're using the **Intl.RelativeTimeFormat** because you want to show text like '3 days ago' and 'in 10 days' in the component.

This next part is a little more complex. The formatter accepts two arguments: a value and what the value represents. If you wanted to show 2 days:

```
this.textContent = formatter.format(2, 'day');
```

Or for last year:

```
this.textContent = formatter.format(-1, 'year');
```

Getting the difference between two dates (today and the provided date) is easy, but changing the resulting difference to be specific to years, months, days and other forms make it a little tougher. Some helper variables will be useful:

```
const secondsToYears = 60 * 60 * 24 * 365;
const secondsToMonths = 60 * 60 * 24 * 30;
```

```
const secondsToDays = 60 * 60 * 24;
const secondsToHours = 60 * 60;
const secondsToMinutes = 60;
```

These will allow you to determine if the difference is greater than the representation and help you to convert the difference into the correct value. Speaking of calculating the difference:

```
const today = new Date();
const diff = (date.getTime() - today.getTime()) / 1000;
const absDiff = Math.abs(diff);
```

The **diff** is calculated by subtracting the number of seconds between the supplied date and today's date (**getTime** returns the value in milliseconds, so dividing it by 1,000 is necessary). To simplify the next part – because it's going to involve determining if a value is greater than each helper variable – the **diff** can't be a negative value, so **Math.abs** takes care of that.

```
let period = 'second';
let value = diff;
```

Both **period** and **value** will change depending of the result of the next part:

```
if (absDiff > secondsToYears) {
  period = 'year';
  value = diff / secondsToYears;
} else if (absDiff > secondsToMonths) {
  period = 'month';
  value = diff / secondsToMonths;
} else if (absDiff > secondsToDays) {
  period = 'day';
  value = diff / secondsToDays;
} else if (absDiff > secondsToHours) {
  period = 'hour';
  value = diff / secondsToHours;
} else if (absDiff > secondsToMinutes) {
  period = 'minute';
```

```
    value = diff / secondsToMinutes;
  }
```

If the **absDiff** (absolute difference) is greater than the helper variable then it's safe to set the **period** and **value**. Finally you can set the element's value:

```
  this.textContent = formatter.format(value, period);
  this.setAttribute('title', date.toISOString());
  }
}
```

Setting the **title** attribute is a nice touch: you could format this too, but for now it's good to show the original date value in the title. To enable the component in your page:

```
customElements.define('time-formatter', TimeFormatter, {
  extends: 'time'
});
```

Instead of seeing a date you should now see a more human-friendly value. Speaking of human-readable, check out this list:

```
  <sentence-list>
    <li>apple</li>
    <li>orange</li>
    <li>banana</li>
  </sentence-list>
```

While a list like this can be useful, sometimes you might prefer to see it as a sentence. This **sentence-list** element also allows for children to be used. Here's how you could write the **render** to take the child elements and output a sentence instead:

```
render() {
  const formatter = new Intl.ListFormat(undefined, {
    style: 'long',
    type: 'conjunction'
  });
```

```
const elements = this.querySelectorAll('li');
const sentence = Array.from(elements).map(
  (el) => el.textContent
);
this.textContent = formatter.format(sentence);
}
```

Which will give you:

- apple, orange and banana

And you don't have to limit yourself to text. You could do the same with a data set: provide the data as attributes and render a chart. Create your own image carousel, calendar, tab or dropdown navigation components. Maybe even the Roman numerals from before as a custom component?

Noise generator

You've heard about white noise generators being able to help some people focus as it helps them to ignore nearby sounds. You have no desire to pay for an app or service that makes unsupported claims, but being an engineer, you enjoy the challenge of making something that you can use for free... and then monetise it later.

Some HTML is needed to play your soon-to-be-generated noise:

```
<!DOCTYPE html>
<html>
  <head>
    <title>Noise generator</title>
  </head>
  <body>
    <audio id="audio" autoplay="false" controls></audio>
    <script src="./noise.js"></script>
  </body>
</html>
```

A setup like this would normally require an audio file to be included with it, but not today. The **controls** attribute is necessary otherwise you won't see the **audio** element. Check what you can see in a browser:

Now you need to get the context:

```
const audioCtx = new (window.AudioContext ||
window.webkitAudioContext)();
const audio = document.getElementById('audio');
const track = audioCtx.createMediaElementSource(audio);
```

The **audioCtx**, **audio** and **track** variables are needed when working with generated audio. This is different to how you'd draw in a **canvas** which uses the **canvas.getContext('2d')**, but it's the same theory: it accesses the underlying audio buffer to add whatever you want.

Before you start generating the audio you need a way to play and pause it. Adding some event listeners will fix that:

```
audio.addEventListener('play', () => {
  // ...
});
audio.addEventListener('pause', () => {
  // ...
});
```

You need to test that the UI works, and while it would be easy to add a **console.log** to the contents of each of the listeners, it would be a little better to hear something:

```
const oscillator = audioCtx.createOscillator();
oscillator.type = 'square';
oscillator.frequency.setValueAtTime(440, audioCtx.currentTime);
oscillator.connect(audioCtx.destination);
```

This **oscillator** is a pre-build generator. With these settings it produces a square wave of 440 Hertz, which is a standard frequency for tuning. If you refresh your browser page now you won't hear anything, even if you click the play/pause button in the **audio** controls. You need to add the **oscillator**'s **start** and **stop** methods to the empty event listeners:

```
audio.addEventListener('play', () => {
  oscillator.start();
});
```

```
audio.addEventListener('pause', () => {
  oscillator.stop();
});
```

Before you press play, *turn the volume down*. Some people find 440 Hertz to be unpleasant at high volume. You can change that to other frequencies: humans can hear between 20 Hz to 20,000 Hz so you have a few options.

But as you can tell this is a consistent sound and not the white noise you might have hoped for. So instead of using the **oscillator**:

```
const bufferSize = audioCtx.sampleRate * 2;
const noiseBuffer = audioCtx.createBuffer(1, bufferSize,
audioCtx.sampleRate);
const output = noiseBuffer.getChannelData(0);
```

The **bufferSize** is the sample rate (which is determined by the browser) multiplied by 2. Why? Because you want to use both left and right channels to hear the audio, so twice as much data is needed in the buffer. This is used for the **noiseBuffer**.

And then there's the **output**. You'll use this to generate your noise. But first:

```
let currentNoise;
const startNoise = () => {
  // ...
};

const stopNoise = () => {
  if (currentNoise) {
    currentNoise.stop();
    currentNoise.disconnect(audioCtx.destination);
    currentNoise = null;
  }
};

audio.addEventListener('play', () => {
  startNoise();
});
audio.addEventListener('pause', () => {
```

```
  stopNoise();
});
```

This is some boilerplate you can use. The contents of the **startNoise** function will be added soon, but like before you need to be able to start and stop the noise.

White noise is nothing more than random values between -1 and 1:

```
const startNoise = () => {
  for (let i = 0; i < bufferSize; i++) {
    output[i] = Math.random() * 2 - 1;
  }

  currentNoise = audioCtx.createBufferSource();
  currentNoise.buffer = noiseBuffer;
  currentNoise.loop = true;
  currentNoise.connect(audioCtx.destination);
  currentNoise.start();
};
```

The **output** will be set using the **bufferSize** in the loop. It will then be used within the **currentNoise** variable as the source, which is then controlled using the **audio** element. You should now be able to play it and hear the noise.

People pay good money to hear that. They pay even more to hear other noise 'colours', like brown and pink. Some refactoring is needed to support that:

```
const startNoise = (type) => {
  switch (type) {
    case 'white':
      for (let i = 0; i < bufferSize; i++) {
        output[i] = Math.random() * 2 - 1;
      }
      break;
```

The addition of the **type** argument and the switch statement are really the only new things here, but they pave the way for the new noises:

```
case 'brown':
  let lastOut = 0.0;
  for (let i = 0; i < bufferSize; i++) {
    const white = Math.random() * 2 - 1;
    const brown = (lastOut + 0.02 * white) / 1.02;
    output[i] = brown * 3.5;
    lastOut = brown;
  }
  break;
```

Brown noise uses the **white** noise from before but manipulates it so it doesn't have the same 'hiss'. It's a simpler noise with a lower pitch that sounds more like a waterfall. For pink noise you need to use Paul Kellet's method[6]:

```
case 'pink':
  let b0, b1, b2, b3, b4, b5, b6;
  b0 = b1 = b2 = b3 = b4 = b5 = b6 = 0.0;
  for (let i = 0; i < bufferSize; i++) {
    const white = Math.random() * 2 - 1;
    b0 = 0.99886 * b0 + white * 0.0555179;
    b1 = 0.99332 * b1 + white * 0.0750759;
    b2 = 0.96900 * b2 + white * 0.1538520;
    b3 = 0.86650 * b3 + white * 0.3104856;
    b4 = 0.55000 * b4 + white * 0.5329522;
    b5 = -0.7616 * b5 - white * 0.0168980;
    output[i] = b0 + b1 + b2 + b3 + b4 + b5 + b6 + white *
0.5362;
    output[i] *= 0.11;
    b6 = white * 0.115926;
  }
  break;
```

Just like before it uses the **white** noise as a seed and modifies it. This is what the three colours look like using the same seed value:

---

[6] https://www.firstpr.com.au/dsp/pink-noise/

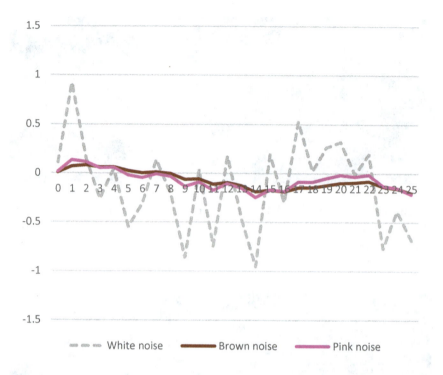

You can see how the brown and pink noises are not as harsh as the white noise. To play them just include the **type** in the **startNoise** function:

```
audio.addEventListener('play', () => {
  startNoise('pink');
});
```

The rest of this is up to you: keep it to yourself, put it behind a paywall or load it up with ads, the choice is yours.

Daily code-breaker

There's a very popular game where a five-letter word is randomly picked and people are given several attempts to solve it (rhymes with hurdle, created by Josh Wardle). After each attempt the picked letters that are in the word are highlighted yellow, and each letter that in the right place is highlighted green.

You've been asked to 'clone' it for a client, but rather than go down the path of lawsuits and expensive penalties for knocking off an original game you've successfully convinced them to change their idea to use a random number (and make a few other alterations).

To start you need to generate that number. Using `Math.random()` sounds like the most effective way, except the number won't be the same for everyone who plays (remember: people like to brag how many attempts they needed to figure out the result). You need a way to make sure everyone gets the same number every 24 hours.

Unlike the original game that uses a dictionary of words to use, you have an advantage by using a number. You can use a seed to generate it:

```
const today = new Date();
const todayNoTime = new Date(
  today.getFullYear(),
  today.getMonth(),
  today.getDate()
);
const seed = todayNoTime.getTime() / 1000;
```

```
console.log(seed);
```

The **seed** variable is today's date in seconds, except it's been set to have no time. This gives your seed a 24-hour window before it changes and as a result you don't need any additional resources like a dictionary.

By using a seed you can then generate a 'random' number. You need this number to be difficult to predict but still usable, so just using the seed isn't good enough. Instead, you need to obfuscate it:

```
const count = 5;
const randomNumber = (() => {
  const x = Math.sin(seed)
    .toString()
    .split('')
    .reverse();

  return x.slice(0, count)
    .join('');
})();

console.log(randomNumber);
```

Using **Math.sin** helps to obfuscate it – by converting the seed into another number and then reversing the order makes it difficult to guess – so this should be fine until someone claims they've 'cracked' your game (there's other trig functions you can use to get different results).

Now that you have the code, you need a way to check it.

```
const checkGuess = (guess) => {
```

First you need to make sure the **guess** meets the criteria of being five numbers. If that isn't met then there's no further checks to do:

```
  if (guess.length !== count) {
    return `Your guess must be ${count} numbers long.`;
  }
  if (guess.match(/[^0-9]/)) {
    return 'Your guess must only contain numbers.';
  }
```

As long as those two checks pass then it's safe to see if the right numbers were entered.

```
const guessArray = guess.split('');
const randomArray = randomNumber.toString().split('');
```

One way to compare the user's code against the generated one is to convert them to arrays. Next you need to check which of them match:

```
const matches = guessArray.filter(
  (char) => randomArray.includes(char)
);

const positionMatches = guessArray.filter(
  (char, index) => char === randomArray[index]
);
```

The **matches** variable will have the correct numbers (without checking the order), and **positionMatches** variable will check to see which numbers are in the correct location.

Now return the result:

```
if (positionMatches.length === 5 &&
    matches.length === 5) {
  return `Well done! You correctly guessed ${randomNumber}.`;
} else {
  return `${matches.length} correct numbers,
${positionMatches.length} in the right place. Please try again.`;
  }
};
```

Playing the game depends on the user interface you plan to use. For this proof-of-concept you can use the browser or the Node command line to test it, but each of them has different ways to prompt the user. *Before* the **checkGuess** function you should add this:

```
const isBrowser = typeof window !== 'undefined';
```

It's a simple check: browsers will return **true** because **window** is valid for them, but a Node server will return **false**. This enables you to take care of both situations:

```
// Input
if (isBrowser) {
  const input = prompt('What is your guess for today?');
  const result = checkGuess(input);
  console.log(result);
} else {
  const readline = require('node:readline')
    .createInterface({
      input: process.stdin,
      output: process.stdout,
    });

  readline.question(
    'What is your guess for today? ',
    (guess) => {
      const result = checkGuess(guess);
      console.log(result);
      readline.close();
    }
  );
}
```

For browsers it will use the **prompt** function, and for Node it will import and setup the necessary **question** instead. When run they will prompt you for today's code and output the **result** once entered.

So what if you wanted it to be a little more like the original and make it visually appealing? The text explanation is good, but colours would be better. To make that happen you need to make some changes to your prompt area:

```
if (isBrowser) {
  const input = prompt('What is your guess for today?');
  const result = checkGuess(input);
  console.log(...result); // <- spread operator
} else {
```

For browsers the `result` is going to return an array so you need to use the spread operator to have it output the text correctly. The next change involves applying styles to the numbers when they're output. After declaring `randomArray` you can add this:

```
if (isBrowser) {
  const colours = [];
  guessArray.forEach((char, index) => {
    if (char === randomArray[index]) {
      colours.push('background:green; color:white;');
    } else if (randomArray.includes(char)) {
      colours.push('background:yellow; color:black;');
    } else {
      colours.push('background:red; color:white;');
    }
  });

  return [
    guessArray.map((num) => `%c${num}`).join(''),
    ...colours
  ];
}
```

When used in a browser you can add some extra characters to `console.log` to control its appearance. For example, if you wanted to show 100% as green text in the console you could use this:

```
console.log('%c100%', 'color: green;');
```

The `%c` tells the console to use the provided style. If you wanted more you can do this:

```
console.log(
  'Traffic lights: %cRed %cAmber %cGreen',
  'color: red;',
  'color: orange;',
  'color: green;'
);
```

Each new style for the corresponding **%c** is an extra argument in the console. Going back to your code: the first value is a string created by prepending a **%c** to each number and the **colours** array containing the styles is spread after it.

This is what it should look like if the first number is in the correct position, the middle numbers are valid but not in their positions, and the last number does not belong:

What is your guess for today? 12345
12345

The browser version is done so Node is next. It's *similar* to the browser except the control codes are not as user-friendly. Something to keep in mind is that when you set the colours for Node's output it will keep using them until you reset it. Start by declaring the **output** and some helper variables:

```
const output = [];
const reset =    '\x1b[0m';
const correct = '\x1b[37m\x1b[42m';
const close =    '\x1b[37m\x1b[43m';
const wrong =    '\x1b[37m\x1b[41m';
```

Similar to **%c** for browsers, the **\x1b** is a control code. Instead of supplying the styles separately Node wants to know what they are straight away, which is why you've declared the styles as their own variables. To finish it off, you can add the rest of the code:

```
guessArray.forEach((char, index) => {
  if (char === randomArray[index]) {
    output.push(`${correct}${char}${reset}`);
  } else if (randomArray.includes(char)) {
    output.push(`${close}${char}${reset}`);
  } else {
    output.push(`${wrong}${char}${reset}`);
  }
});
return output.join('');
};
```

Just like before: if the number is in the correct position it's styled green, yellow if it's in the array and red if it's not. It should return the output as a string and will look the same as the browser version.

The `${correct}${char}${reset}` pattern helps to keep the code a little cleaner. You could just make it looks like this:

```
output.push(`\x1b[37m\x1b[42m${char}\x1b[0m`);
```

But that might not be helpful in a few weeks (or months/years) when you have to do some refactoring. At least by using those control codes in variables makes it more readable for you.

And that's it! You now have a game that generates a random-looking number for players to try and guess that resets every day. Except there's one more feature that's missing: you need to limit the number of attempts. Start by determining how many attempts you want to give the player (near the top of the file, like near `isBrowser`, should be fine):

```
const attempts = [];
const maxAttempts = 5;
```

Because you're counting it might be nice to see the number of attempts, like 1st, 2nd and 3rd. This can be done with an ordinal helper function:

```
const ordinal = (number) => {
  const lastDigit = number % 10;
  const lastTwoDigits = number % 100;
  if (lastTwoDigits >= 11 && lastTwoDigits <= 13) {
    return `${number}th`;
  }
  switch (lastDigit) {
    case 1:
      return `${number}st`;
    case 2:
      return `${number}nd`;
    case 3:
      return `${number}rd`;
    default:
      return `${number}th`;
```

```
    }
};
```

That's nice, but there's a better way to do that:

```
const pluralRules = new Intl.PluralRules(undefined, { type:
'ordinal' });
const suffixes = new Map([
  ['one', 'st'],
  ['two', 'nd'],
  ['few', 'rd'],
  ['other', 'th'],
]);
const ordinal = (number) => {
  const rule = pluralRules.select(number);
  const suffix = suffixes.get(rule);
  return `${number}${suffix}`;
};
```

`Intl.PluralRules` is a built-in internationalisation class that can help: in this case you can use the rules for plurals to determine the `suffix` for the `number`. Using this is slightly less code than the original `ordinal` function but is a lot simpler because it handles the logic for you.

The biggest problem is that to get the prompt you need to run the script, but then it stops asking for more guesses. To begin to fix this you need to change what the `checkGuess` function returns:

```
if (isBrowser) {
  ...
  attempts.push(guess);
  return {
    isComplete: guess === randomNumber,
    output: [
      guessArray.map((num) => `%c${num}`).join(''),
      ...colours
    ]
  };
}
```

The **output** is the same, but **isComplete** and the push for the new attempt/s is new. A similar update is needed for the Node version:

```
attempts.push(guess);
return {
  isComplete: guess === randomNumber,
  output: output.join(''),
};
```

You don't want to keep redeclaring the **readline** variable when using Node, so that should be moved out of the prompt condition:

```
let readline;
if (!isBrowser) {
  readline = require('node:readline').createInterface({
    input: process.stdin,
    output: process.stdout,
  });
}
```

And now for the **promptPlayer** function to replace the code after the **checkGuess** function:

```
// Input
const promptPlayer = () => {
  if (attempts.length >= maxAttempts) {
    console.log(
      `The number was ${randomNumber}. You had ${maxAttempts}
attempts. Better luck tomorrow!`
    );
    return;
  }
```

This checks if the number of attempts – if the player has reached the maximum number of attempts (**maxAttempts**) then you should let them see what the answer was.

```
const attempt = ordinal(attempts.length + 1);
const message = `What is your ${attempt} guess? `;
```

Updating the message to show which attempt the player is at helps to keep them focussed and prepares them for the next.

```
if (isBrowser) {
  const input = prompt(message);
  const result = checkGuess(input);
  console.log(...result.output);
  if (result.isComplete) {
    console.log(`You win! ${attempts.length} attempts.`);
    return;
  }
  promptPlayer();
```

You still **output** the `result` to the **console**, but now there's a check to see if the guess is complete. Otherwise, prompt them again.

The Node version follows similar logic except you need to **close** the **readline** when it's not needed anymore.

```
} else {
  readline.question(message, (guess) => {
    const result = checkGuess(guess);
    console.log(result.output);
    if (result.isComplete) {
      console.log(`You win! ${attempts.length} attempts.`);
      readline.close();
      return;
    }
    promptPlayer();
    if (attempts.length >= maxAttempts) {
      readline.close();
    }
  });
}
};
```

And now it's time to start the prompting:

```
promptPlayer();
```

Now the player has five attempts to guess the code. But what happens if the player doesn't like not winning? They could just refresh the browser and keep trying. You need a way to preserve the information: caching the attempts could be a good idea, which leads into the next project.

Caching

Things like databases and other kinds of storage are beyond the scope of this book, but sometimes you need to quickly save some values for later and that's where caching comes in handy.

To make caching work you need to determine if the system is working in a browser or server (Node) and then make sure the same API is available that 'just handles it' (if you're working exclusively in one of the other just omit the condition you're not using). Caches are usually managed through keys and expiration times – the keys let you get and set the data, but if it expires then it needs to be removed.

You're also going to use a class for this. The reason is because it helps with scope: each method that uses the cache should not be able to touch other caches: you want to keep them contained.

```
class CustomCache {
```

You can call a class anything though it's generally preferred for it to start with a capital letter. Next is the constructor:

```
constructor() {
    this.isBrowser = typeof window !== 'undefined' &&
window.localStorage;
    if (this.isBrowser) {
        this.cache = window.localStorage;
    } else {
```

```
    this.cache = {};
  }
}
```

The **constructor** is run when the class is initialised. Here you've used **isBrowser** again and that can be used to make sure the correct code paths are used. The API for this class needs to perform the following tasks, nearly all of which will accept a **key** as an argument:

- set: create or update the value using its key
- get: retrieve the value by its key
- del: remove the key and value (delete is a reserved word in JavaScript)
- has: check if the key is valid
- flushAll: remove everything

```
set(key, value, ttl = 24 * 60 * 60) {
  const data = {
    value,
    expiration: Date.now() + ttl * 1000
  };

  if (this.isBrowser) {
    this.cache.setItem(key, JSON.stringify(data));
  } else {
    this.cache[key] = data;
  }
}
```

The **set** function in the cache class accepts three arguments: **key**, **value** and **ttl** (or time-to-live) that has a default value of one day (24 hours * 60 minutes * 60 seconds). The **data** object uses both the value and an **expiration** date based on the **ttl** value – when the expiration is less than the current date then the cached key and value needs to be removed.

If the class is used in a browser, it will use the **localStorage**'s **setItem**, otherwise the default cache object is used. When using **localStorage** the key/value pairs can only be stored as strings so **JSON.stringify** is needed to convert the data object. Now to get the cached data:

```
get(key) {
  const item = this.isBrowser
    ? JSON.parse(this.cache.getItem(key))
    : this.cache[key];

  if (item && item.expiration > Date.now()) {
    return item.value;
  }
  // Remove expired (or non-existent) item
  this.del(key);

  return undefined;
}
```

Just like before the method of retrieval depends on whether it's in the browser or server (parsing the string back to JSON if it's the browser). This is where the **expiration** check happens too: if it's greater than the current date then the **value** can be returned, otherwise it has to be removed.

Now to get rid of the value:

```
del(key) {
  if (this.isBrowser) {
    this.cache.removeItem(key);
  } else {
    delete this.cache[key];
  }
}
```

Use the **removeItem** for **localStorage**, otherwise **delete** the **key** from the **cache**. Last two methods:

```
has(key) {
  return !!this.get(key) &&
    this.get(key).expiration > Date.now();
}

flushAll() {
  if (this.isBrowser) {
```

```
    this.cache.clear();
  } else {
    this.cache = {};
  }
 }
}
```

Using your cache class is similar to declaring every other variable in JavaScript:

```
const myCache = new CustomCache();
```

The **myCache** variable (again, name it whatever you want) now has all the methods needed to operate a cache, so if you wanted to set a value:

```
const key = 'myKey';
const value = 'myValue';
const ttl = 60; // 60 seconds
myCache.set(key, value, ttl);
```

And to get it:

```
const cachedValue = myCache.get(key);
console.log(cachedValue); // myValue
```

And if you wait more than 60 seconds, the value will be gone!

Quick comment

Using this cache in the browser is easy: just make sure it's **import**ed, **require**d or loaded in some way *before* you declare it – the class handles the rest. Node is a different story: because it's a server the cached values aren't limited to just one user. A cached value on a server could be available to *everyone* on it.

You also need to be careful where the cache is declared: if it's for a single script/page/route or inside a function then the cache will be redeclared each time it loads. If you prefer the cache to persist over time you need to make sure it's declared during the initial setup.

Linear regression

What's the next number in this sequence: 1, 2, 3, 4, 5? If you guessed 6 then you'd be correct. What about 3, 6, 9, 12, 15? Yep, 18 is correct.

Now try 1, 2, 7, 9 and 10.

Or 210, 753, 1000, 1235 and 1973?

It's not easy to work with those last two sequences to determine the next number. But there is a solution: linear regression, or 'line of best fit'.

You start by getting those values into an array, starting with the first sequence because you already know the answer:

```
const data = [1, 2, 3, 4, 5];
```

Linear regression needs two things: the values that you already have and a scale to measure them. The data you have could be represented as values on a y-axis of a chart, and the scale would be the x-axis.

You don't have a scale, so let's keep it simple and generate one:

```
const xyData = data.map((y, x) => ({
  x,
  y,
}));
```

Your data **y** now has a relationship to an **x** value (remember the second argument of **map** is an index-0 integer). The data has been transformed and is ready for some more math:

```
[
  { x: 0, y: 1 },
  { x: 1, y: 2 },
  { x: 2, y: 3 },
  { x: 3, y: 4 },
  { x: 4, y: 5 },
];
```

So why is it necessary to give it **x** and **y** values? This is what the data looks like when plotted as a chart:

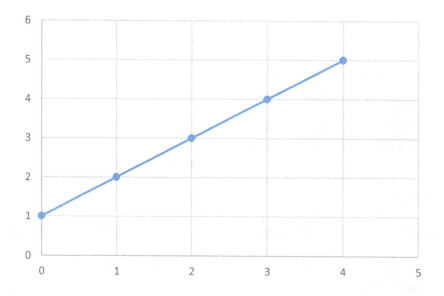

The line that connects the dots represents that **x/y** relationship. And if you know what that line is doing now, you can predict the next value (yes, you know it's 6 but the code doesn't).

To do that, you need: the sum of all the **x** values, the sum of all the **y** values, the sum of each **x** value multiplied by its **y** value, and lastly the sum of the **x** value multiplied by itself.

You can reduce the **xyData** like this:

```
const sums = xyData.reduce(
  (acc, { x, y }) => {
    acc.x += x;
```

```
    acc.y += y;
    acc.xy += x * y;
    acc.xx += x * x;
    return acc;
  },
  { x: 0, y: 0, xy: 0, xx: 0 }
);
```

And that makes this:

```
{
  x: 10,
  xx: 30,
  xy: 40,
  y: 15
}
```

Why is this data needed? Because linear regression works by determining the gradient (direction and steepness) of the data and using this equation:

$$y = mx + b$$

The next value **y** can be calculated when you know the gradient (**m**), the next **x** value and the intercept (**b**).

For the gradient you need to do this (also known as the Least Squares Method):

-   calculate the *numerator* by multiplying the sum of the **x+y** calculations you did earlier with the number of values and subtract the sum of the **x** values multiplied by the sum of the y values
-   calculate the *denominator* by multiplying the sum of the squared **x** calculations you did earlier with the number of values and subtract the sum of the **x** values multiplied by itself
-   divide the *numerator by the denominator*

In JavaScript it looks like this (and may be easier to understand):

```
const count = xyData.length;
const gradient = (count * sums.xy - sums.x * sums.y) /
                 (count * sums.xx - sums.x * sums.x);
```

The **count** is easy: it's just the length of the array. It's the **gradient** that might give you some trouble, so let's break it down using the values calculated from the **sums** object:

- count = 5
- sum of x = 10
- sum of y = 15
- sum of xy = 40
- sum of xx = 30
- numerator = 5 * 40 – 10 * 15
   - 200 – 150
   - 50
- denominator = 5 * 30 – 10 * 10
   - 150 – 100
   - 50
- gradient = 50 / 50
   - 1

This gives you a gradient of 1. For the values of 1, 2, 3, 4 and 5 that's correct, but this will change when other values are used or if the time scale is different.

The intercept is another calculation but it's a bit easier: the average/mean of the **y** values subtracted by the gradient multiplied by the mean of the **x** values, or:

```
const intercept = (sums.y / count) - gradient * (sums.x / count);
```

- intercept = 15 / 5 – 1 * 10 / 5
   - 3 – 1 * 2
   - 3 – 2
   - 1

The **intercept** sounds complicated, but it's just a number that represents what the **y** will be when **x = 0** (check the chart). That's why it's added at the end of the equation (**b**). To finish this so you can predict the next value you need to complete the original equation:

$$y = mx + b$$

```
const nextX = xyData[count - 1].x + 1;
const nextY = gradient * nextX + intercept;
```

The next x value will be 5 (index-0 remember) so:

- y = gradient * 5 + intercept
- y = 1 * 5 + 1
    - ○ 6

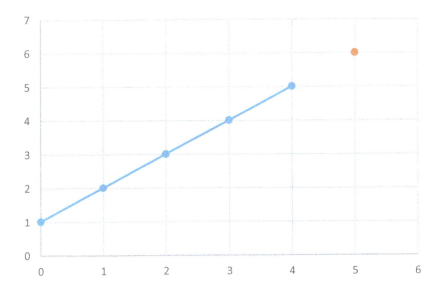

All that effort to figure out the next number after 1, 2, 3, 4 and 5 is 6? Now try those other sequences:

```
const data = [1, 2, 7, 9, 10];
```

The next 'best fit' value in the sequence will be 13.3.

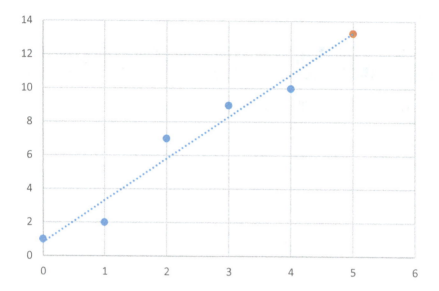

There's a lot more you could do here: the **x** values were generated, but real data will be dates and times (you could convert those into a Unix timestamp and use those values for your **x** axis attributes), and it's likely those won't be as uniform as the index used.

But that's not a problem: the gradient and intercept will change as the values do, so as long as you use the correct **x** value when calculating the **y** then you won't have to make any changes.

To prove this, you could make an adjustment to the **xyData** generator to add 10 when **x** is more than 2 so you could see what a jump in the time scale would do:

```
const xyData = data.map((y, x) => ({
  x: x > 2 ? x + 10 : x,
  y,
}));
```

Which alters the data:

```
[
  { x: 0, y: 1 },
  { x: 1, y: 2 },
  { x: 2, y: 3 },
  { x: 13, y: 4 },
```

```
{ x: 14, y: 5 }
];
```

Your original **y** values haven't changed but there's a jump in the **x** values. For this sequence the next number is 4.89. It's less than before because it's extending the line of best fit: the gradient is less than earlier and the intercept is different too.

This value might seem wrong, but this is one of the downsides of linear regression: it's only as accurate as your data. That jump introduced errors the same way 1, 2, 7, 9 and 10 on the **y** axis, assuming you wanted the next value. If you knew these jumps in time were occurring then you wouldn't worry about the very next value, instead you'd want to predict the 20th or 30th value as they would be more accurate.

Hashcash

There are various cryptocurrencies that uses a proof-of-work system to confirm that a transaction has occurred. One of them is called Hashcash.

A similar Hashcash system was used to limit email spam: it was additional work for the sender to complete. That work was more *expensive* than the email itself (time is money), so it was an effective way to help filter out unwanted messages.

The filter used by the receiver was quick because of the way Hashcash results worked: the amount of computational time needed to check the work was negligible, but the amount of time needed to complete the original work was huge.

Think of it like a postage stamp to send a letter: it costs the sender but is quick for others to see that it was done.

You're now going to build your own Hashcash system. To start you need to know:

- The version
- Number of bits to test
- The date
- Who it's being sent to
- The extension (not used anymore)
- A random number
- A counter

And here's the code:

```
const version = 1;
const bits = 20;
const date = new Date().toISOString().slice(0, 10);
const resource = 'user@example.com';
const extension = '';
const rand = Math.random().toString(36);
const counter = 0;

const hashcash =
`${version}:${bits}:${date}:${resource}:${extension}:${rand}:${co
unter}`;
console.log(hashcash);
// 1:20:2023-12-31:user@example.com::0.05k8fa4yh1yg:0
```

Let's rewind a little. That code won't produce a valid Hashcash because it hasn't done any real work. The work occurs with the **rand** variable, and it has to fulfill very specific requirements.

Hashcash works by taking a string and hashing it - hashing is a mathematical process where the input is converted to a different value, however unlike encryption it can't be reversed. The work won't stop until the beginning digits of the hash (see the **bit** variable) are all **0**. After each failed attempt it creates a new **rand** value and increments the **counter**. This is a brute-force process: it will keep trying until it gets it.

So that's what you need to do. How about you reset those variables:

```
const version = 1;
const bits = 4; // Multiple of 4
const date = new Date().toISOString().slice(0, 10);
const resource = 'user@example.com';
const info = '';
let counter = 0;
```

The **info** variable has replaced the original **extension**, but you can use it to store other information (or keep it blank, up to you). Now to generate the Hashcash string:

```
const makeHashcashString = () => {
  const rand = btoa(Math.random().toString(36));
  counter++;
```

```
  return
`${version}:${bits}:${date}:${resource}:${info}:${rand}:${counter
}`;
}
```

Every time the **makeHashcashString** function is called it:

- creates a new string of random data (**rand**),
- increments the global **counter** and
- returns the string

The **btoa()** function converts your random data into Base64 – it's possible for the random data to include characters other than letters and numbers, and you'll be relying on those colons (**:**) separating the data. Better safe than sorry.

Next is the function to convert that string into a hash. The latest version of JavaScript supports the Crypto interface. It's short for Cryptography (not cryptocurrency) and allows you to use some advanced and very secure technology to hash the data. Unfortunately, it's a Promise.

The **makeHashcashString** function is a synchronous function, meaning it prevents anything else from running while it does its thing. This is normal JavaScript behaviour. Promises are asynchronous: they start something and everything else can continue, and when they're finished, they let you know. These Promises are great for functions like fetching data from a server because you want to do other things while waiting for it to load.

Everything in the Crypto interface returns Promises, which means you need to use an **async** function:

```
const convertToHash = async (input) => {
  const encoder = new TextEncoder();
  const data = encoder.encode(input);
  const hashBuffer = await crypto.subtle.digest(
    'SHA-256', data
  );
  const hashArray = Array.from(
    new Uint8Array(hashBuffer)
  );
  const hashHex = hashArray
    .map((byte) => byte.toString(16).padStart(2, '0'))
```

```
    .join('');

    return hashHex;
};
```

The **async** and **await** are often used when dealing with Promises. That **hashBuffer** must wait for the **crypto** method to finish before it can continue. The **async** is used on the surrounding function. You'll be using it a few times here.

The **convertToHash** function does several things:

- Encodes your Hashcash **input** to **data**
- Loads the SHA-256 hashing function and mathematically transforms the **data**
- Converts the buffer information into an array
- Maps each 'byte' in the array into a hexadecimal value
    - o   And adds some padding if necessary
- Returns the new hash string

All that work to get a string that looks like this:

- 28a2da3b5a1369e5f7bf3df55957dbf3ccf93c7ef0776805eefce57c7b556a6c

Here's a quick test: a valid hash in this exercise will start with two **0**s. Does this hash pass? No. It starts with **28**, not **00**.

Checking for a valid hash is very quick, so writing a validation function to check that the hash is valid for both the user creating it and the person/system receiving it would be a good idea. It also uses the function you just wrote:

```
const validate = async (hashcash) => {
  const [version, bits, date, resource, info, rand, counter] =
    hashcash.split(':');
  const hash = await convertToHash(hashcash);
  const bytes = parseInt(bits, 10) / 4;
  const matchZeroes = new Array(bytes).fill('0').join('');

  if (hash.slice(0, bytes) !== matchZeroes) {
    return false;
  }
}
```

```
  return true;
};
```

First thing the function needs to know it how many bits it should be checking for. That comes from the Hashcash string, you just have to `split` it and get the `bits` value.

Then you need to use the `convertToHash` function you just wrote. This is an `async/await` function which means your validator will also be an `async` function. Now that you have the `hash` it needs to check the number of `0`s.

The `matchZeros` is generated based on the number of `bytes` (character bytes are 4 bits each), so if you had a 20-bit hash challenge it would look for `00000` at the start of the hash. As you're testing this the current bit variable is set to 4, so just one `0` needs to be found.

If the first character in the hash isn't a `0`, then the hash isn't valid. If it is valid then it will `return true`.

You want to see this work? Time for the final function:

```
const compute = async () => {
  let hashcash = makeHashcashString();
  let hash = await convertToHash(hashcash);
  let valid = await validate(hashcash);
  console.log(hashcash);
  console.log(hash);
  console.log(valid);
};

compute();
```

Don't forget that `compute()` function call at the end. This is what your output will look like:

- `1:4:2009-01 03:user@example.com::MC5hanpxMnRzMXM2cw==:1`
- `1c3506cfbfb86e64a3bf3b56d19eee782f6d29b812f882a0f75f749f859bc34a`
- `false`

You can see the version number, bits, date, email, random data and the counter. You can also see it failed the verification check. So how do you run it until the check passes? A loop is ideal, but remember this is a computationally heavy process, and you're still testing it, so you'll want to see what's happening.

Instead you can use a timer interval. It's not a loop, but it can be used like one and it handles those Promises too. Here's an updated version of the compute function:

```
const compute = async () => {
  let valid = false;
  let hash = '';
  let hashcash = '';

  const timer = setInterval(async () => {
    hashcash = makeHashcashString();
    hash = await convertToHash(hashcash);
    valid = await validate(hashcash);
    console.log(hash)
    if (valid) {
      clearInterval(timer);
      console.log('complete', hashcash, hash);
    }
  }, 100);
};
```

Every 100 milliseconds the code will run and when the hash is valid it will stop. Using a timer adds a delay to the process, but it will be worthwhile in a moment. Check that the **bits** variable is still **4**, then let it run.

- 1:4:2023-12-31:user@example.com::MC4xajkwZTduZTZ2Mw==:65
- 017f3efda6e4a7d77ef09e13f2c1c81e9690d3be9b986bd3984ab1c3303310e6

That 65 at the end means it took 65 attempts to find a hash with a single **0** at the start. Do you want to see what it takes for two **0**s? Update the **bits** and let it run.

```
const bits = 8; // Multiple of 4
```

- 1:8:2023-12-31:user@example.com::MC40YXdkcW500XNmMw==:212
- 007859c1f1cfe6cffeb3da9f987fe9fa912562611512ab84c348d433e9cb64ed

212 attempts! This is what makes Hashcash so computationally expensive:

it keeps trying random values until the validation returns **true**. The functions that create and validate the hash are quick, but it's the brute-force process that takes time.

If you're seeing similar results then it means you've successfully created a Hashcash system. If you want to increase the number of bits or reduce the timer interval to see more results then go ahead. Just know that increasing the **bits** makes the process take longer, and as you've see finding a hash with one **0** is *a lot* faster than finding one with five.

Linear regression using machine learning

Many people might say that JavaScript is not the right language for machine learning. But don't let that stop you. Your linear regression system from earlier in the book works well (i.e. it gives you the answers) so let's use it to jump into machine learning.

In 2024 computers *still* use binary at the hardware level to calculate everything: colours, buttons, functions, all of that. As a result they're great at performing maths very quickly, but learning to do something new isn't a task they can do by default.

The majority of machine learning is about the training: reinforcing when something is correct and forgetting what's incorrect. You're going to create a new version of the linear regression analysis that learns over time to calculate the next number based on previous values. Instead of calculating the gradient and intercept you'll instead *train* the model to do it for you. To get started you need to bring back some familiar variables:

```
let m = 0;
let b = 0;
```

As you can see with **m** as your gradient and **b** as the intercept, they're both at 0. You're going to train it to figure out what they should be. For this project they will be available in the global scope and available to all functions (as they're using **let** they can changed by different things too).

You should now determine your learning rate:

```
const lr = 0.01;
```

```
const epochs = 1000;
```

The learning rate determines if information should be retained or forgotten. Each epoch, or a single act of 'learning' using all the training data, is how the model learns. Here's your training data:

```
const data = [
  { x: 0, y: 1 },
  { x: 1, y: 2 },
  { x: 2, y: 3 },
  { x: 3, y: 4 },
  { x: 4, y: 5 }
];
```

From this data you need to extract the *inputs* and *outputs*. For this situation the inputs are the x values (the values you start with) and the outputs are the y values (the values you want). These should be separate arrays:

```
const inputs = [];
const outputs = [];
data.forEach((item) => {
  inputs.push(item.x);
  outputs.push(item.y);
});
```

To train the model you need to take each of the x values in the `inputs` array and demonstrate what needs to happen to convert them to their corresponding y values. Remember the equation from earlier?

$$y = mx + b$$

It needs to be a function:

```
const predict = (x) => m * x + b;
```

During the training the same code needs to be run repeatedly. Unlike the previous hashcash example that wouldn't stop until it found the right hash, using epochs determines how many times the model should be trained. During each training session the following will be run:

- For each of the inputs:
  - o Make a prediction using the current input
  - o Compare the prediction against the output
  - o Calculate the gradient and intercept
  - o Update the model

This requires two loops, one inside the other:

```
for (let i = 0; i < epochs; i++) {
  for (let i = 0; i < inputs.length; i++) {
```

Now to make the predictions. Keep in mind that right now both **m** and **b** equal **0**, so the first prediction is going to be completely wrong. The good thing is that it will learn and get better.

```
const pred = predict(inputs[i]);
```

Next is to calculate the gradients. Not the gradient (**m**) that you want the model to learn, but the gradient of the loss between your input and output values.

```
const dm = -2 * (outputs[i] - pred) * inputs[i];
const db = -2 * (outputs[i] - pred);
```

It's a mathematical way of telling the model how wrong it was when it made its prediction. Let's manually calculate this to make it easier:

```
-   m = 0
-   b = 0
-   x = inputs[i] = 0
-   y = outputs[i] = 1
-   prediction = m * x + b
    o  0 * 0 + 0
    o  0
```

The **dm** and **db** are found like this:

```
-  dm = -2 * (1 - 0) * 0
   o  -2 * 1 * 0
```

$$db = -2 * (1 - 0)$$
- $\circ$ -2 * 1
- $\circ$ -2

These values are the derivatives of the Mean Squared Error (MSE) loss function. If the difference between the actual result and the predicted one is significant then the MSE will be large and result in more changes for the next epoch (reinforcement). As the difference reduces so too does the MSE and this results in less reinforcement.

Finally, you need to update the model values and apply the learning rate (and finish off the loops):

```
m -= lr * dm;
b -= lr * db;

}
}
```

A single pass doesn't do much, but if run the same code several times with just the first input/output pairs then the values begin to change:

m	b	prediction	dm	db
0	0	0	0	-2
0	0.02	0.02	0	-1.96
0	0.0396	0.0396	0	-1.9208
0	0.058808	0.058808	0	-1.88238
0	0.077632	0.077632	0	-1.84474

After 100 epochs you can see the **b** get larger while its derivative gets closer to **0**. Each time this happens less changes are made to the model because the predictions are getting more accurate:

m	b	prediction	dm	db
0	0.864673923	0.864673923	0	-0.270652155

After 1,000 epochs of training the model is a lot more certain:

m	b	prediction	dm	db
0	0.999999998	0.999999998	0	-0.00000000343463

The **db** has become too small to have any major impact on the predicted gradient. As this is done with all the input/output pairs they will be even more accurate than what's calculated here.

By now the **m** and **b** values will have changed and will no longer be **0**. So how can you predict the next value in the sequence? By using the same **predict** function with a new **x** value:

```
const result = predict(5);
console.log(result); // 6.000000000000014
```

Close enough to 6. What about the other data from before?

```
const data = [
  { x: 0, y: 3 },
  { x: 1, y: 6 },
  { x: 2, y: 9 },
  { x: 3, y: 12 },
  { x: 4, y: 15 }
];

const result = predict(5);
console.log(result); // 18.000000000000043
```

And this one:

```
const data = [
  { x: 0, y: 1 },
  { x: 1, y: 2 },
  { x: 2, y: 7 },
  { x: 3, y: 9 },
  { x: 4, y: 10 }
];

const result = predict(5);
console.log(result); // 13.026870121378826
```

It's not the same 13.3 from last time, but close enough. Because of the training it's not going to be perfect: the variable values that change the model became too small to have much of an impact. As a result the gradient and intercept aren't exactly the same as the original linear regression model:

```
m = 1.0000000000000078
b = 0.999999999999756
```

Changing the number of epochs or the learning rate will impact the training, and unfortunately there's no *ideal* number for them:

- Not enough epochs = not enough training
- Too many epochs = gradients could explode or vanish
- Learning rate too high = the model (**m** and **b**) might overshoot their ideal value
- Learning rate too low = the model will never get to the ideal value

To know if some tweaking needs to be made it's a good idea to determine the loss. You can add this function before the loops:

```
const loss = (pred, target) => Math.pow(
  pred - target, 2
);
```

You used the derivative of the MSE for the **dm** and **db**: the loss function is the Mean Square Error itself.

```
for (let i = 0; i < epochs; i++) {
  let totalLoss = 0;
  for (let i = 0; i < inputs.length; i++) {
    const pred = predict(inputs[i]);

    // Calculate the loss
    const l = loss(pred, outputs[i]);
    totalLoss += l;

    const dm = -2 * (outputs[i] - pred) * inputs[i];
    const db = -2 * (outputs[i] - pred);

    m -= lr * dm;
    b -= lr * db;
```

```
    }

    // Show the loss
    console.log(`Epoch ${i}: Loss = ${totalLoss / inputs.length}`);
}
```

You'll get something like this when you run the code again:

```
Epoch 0: Loss = 7.243587510733972
Epoch 1: Loss = 1.6545080510647872
Epoch 2: Loss = 0.44145011238125437
Epoch 3: Loss = 0.17010848404290432
...
Epoch 997: Loss = 2.434153582575873e-28
Epoch 998: Loss = 2.2617628228817933e-28
Epoch 999: Loss = 2.172448977268802e-28
```

Big losses in the beginning but it's quick to recover. In the last epoch the losses are so very small the model is not going to change much (e^{-28} means you need to move that decimal 28 places to the left – it's a lot of zeros). But if you increase the learning rate:

```
const lr = 0.2;
```

This is what happens:

```
Epoch 0: Loss = 3.3271086079999934
Epoch 1: Loss = 64.42924010064299
Epoch 2: Loss = 1389.3137014014894
...
Epoch 229: Loss = 1.876327377439958e+305
Epoch 230: Loss = 4.020510079523057e+306
Epoch 231: Loss = Infinity
Epoch 232: Loss = Infinity
```

The learning rate is too high: instead of a gradual reduction in the loss this learning rate caused a massive increase and as a result will never come close to the ideal. Being able to see the losses will help you to fine-tune the training to get better results.

Clickbait detector using Naïve Bayes classifier

Some people seem to think that clickbait headlines are a great idea to promote traffic and engagement to their sites. Both you and your client disagree, which is why you want to write system to determine if an article should be labelled as click-bait or a regular headline.

When it comes to labelling (or classifying) text a Naïve Bayes classifier is the way to go. It's a simple but effective technique and as you'll be working with text is an ideal way to help show the basics of machine learning classifiers.

Clickbait is supposed to grab people's attention so it's frequently used as the heading or title of an article or blog (and some 'news' articles). Ideally you would want a greater list of headlines to help classify them, but for now you can use some basic training data:

```
const trainingData = {
  'clickbait': [
    'you won\'t believe this',
    'this is the best thing ever',
    'simple rules to',
    'you\'ll never guess',
    'the last one blew my mind',
    'you\'ll never believe what'
  ],
  'headline': [
    'local team celebrates',
```

```
    'economic forecast looks bleak',
    'simple rules for winter',
    'the election was last week',
    'the new movie is out',
    'the new restaurant downtown'
  ]
};
```

Right now there's two classifications – or classes: **click-bait** and **headline**. You could always adapt these later to classify other headlines – like economics, sports, and social – but for early development you can stick with these two.

Now that you have the **trainingData** it's time to write some helper functions, and the first one is for training:

```
const classes = {};

const train = (data, label) => {
  if (!classes[label]) {
    classes[label] = [];
  }
  classes[label].push(data.split(' '));
};
```

After processing the **trainingData** the **classes** will look almost identical except that the **data** has been **split** at every space. The reason for the **split** is to help when you're going to determine the probability of the incoming headline matching one of the pre-learned headlines. Why the extra processing to get almost the same thing as the training data? Because you may need to perform extra work like converting the strings to lowercase, cleaning the values or removing keywords to get a better result.

In order to predict if an incoming headline is clickbait you need to determine how well it 'matches' against the data in each class. That's where this function is needed:

```
const probability = (classData, data) => {
  let p = 1;
  classData.forEach((val, i) => {
    p *= data[i] === val ? 0.65 : 0.35;
```

```
});
  return p;
};
```

The **probability** function does the heavy lifting here. By looping through each item in the supplied **classData** (**class** is a reserved word which is why you didn't use it) and then determining how well it matches the **data** headline. It then returns the probability of the headline being in that class.

Let's say the incoming headline is '10 simple rules to make this summer better'. If the words for each training headline and incoming headline are at the same index then the probability (**p**) is multiplied by a certain factor (**0.65** if it's more-likely, **0.35** if it's less likely).

To show you what the results look like, here's the probabilities:

Clickbait class		
Training data	*Headline*	*Probability*
you won't believe this		0.015006249999999995
this is the best thing ever		0.0018382656249999992
simple rules to	10 simple rules to make this summer better	**0.04287499999999999**
you'll never guess		**0.04287499999999999**
the last one blew my mind		0.00183826562499999
you'll never believe what		0.01500624999999999

Compare that against the Headline class:

Headline class		
Training data	*Headline*	*Probability*
local team celebrates		**0.04287499999999999**
economic forecast looks bleak		0.015006249999999995
simple rules for winter	10 simple rules to make this summer better	0.015006249999999995
the election was last week		0.005252187499999998
the new movie is out		0.005252187499999998
the new restaurant downtown		0.015006249999999995

Both classes return high probabilities across three of the trained headlines (the ones in **bold**). You might have noticed that 'you'll never guess' and 'local team celebrates' returned high probabilities despite not having any of the words. That's from the small number of the trained headlines: there aren't enough words to reduce the probability which is why it's important to have reliable training data. You'll be fixing this bug later.

Now that you have a training function it's time to feed it the data:

```
Object.keys(trainingData).map((key) => {
  trainingData[key].forEach((data) => train(data, key));
});
```

It's two loops: the first to loop through each `key` in the `trainingData` object and the next to `train` it. To predict if the headline is clickbait or not:

```
const predict = (data) => {
  let max = -Infinity;
  let maxClass = null;
  for (let c in classes) {
    let p = 0;
    classes[c].forEach((d) => {
      p += probability(d, data.split(' '));
    });
    if (p > max) {
      max = p;
      maxClass = c;
    }
  }
  return maxClass;
};
```

Remember the `probability` function? Because it returns a larger sum of probabilities from the clickbait class it determines that the headline (`data`) is clickbait.

Naïve Bayes classifiers are a family of techniques but they all share the same behaviour: each *thing* they compare is independent of every other *thing*. For the approach you're using each word, when compared against other words, are done so regardless of which word came before or after. It also means similar words like 'rules' and 'rule' are considered different when used to calculate the final probability.

```
console.log(predict('10 simple rules to make this summer
better'));
// clickbait
console.log(predict('local team wins by 10'));
// headline
```

The short headings in **trainingData** have reduced the effectiveness of this classifier, so more accurate headings are needed. These headings also need to be specific so that patterns can be found:

```
const trainingData = {
  clickbait: [
    'Unbelievable! This AI Predicts Your Future Career Based on
Your Watching Habits!',
    'Incredible! This AI Predicts Your Past Life Based on Your
Watching Habits!',
    'Amazing! This AI Predicts Your Future Partner Based on Your
Watching Habits!',
    'Unbelievable! This AI Predicts Your Dream Car Based on Your
Watching Habits!',
    'Stunning! This AI Predicts Your Dream Job Based on Your
Watching Habits!'
  ],
  headline: [
    'Research indicates promising results in slowing Alzheimer\'s
progression',
    'Study indicates potential cognitive benefits of daily brain
exercises',
    'Clinical study indicates significant results in slowing
Alzheimer\'s progression',
    'Research finds promising results in slowing Alzheimer\'s
progression',
    'Donor support critical to Alzheimer\'s research progress',
  ]
};
```

There are only a few words of difference between each headline in each class, but it's easier to see the pattern between the two.

The headlines need to be cleaned too: those capitals and exclamation marks will change the probabilities and will reduce how effective you classifier can be (**'Research'** is not the same as **'research'**):

```
const clean = (data) => {
  return data
    .toLowerCase()
    .replace(/[^a-z0-9\s]/g, '')
    .split(' ');
};
```

You'll also need to update your **train** and **predict** functions to use the **clean** function:

```
const train = (data, label) => {
  // ...
  const words = clean(data);
  classes[label].push(words);
};
```

```
const predict = (data) => {
  let max = -Infinity;
  let maxClass = null;
  // ...
    classes[c].forEach((d) => {
      p += probability(d, clean(data));
    });
```

Now if you use the headlines the accuracy of your classifier will improve:

```
console.log(predict('Unbelievable! This App Predicts Your Past
Life Based on Your Habits!'));
// clickbait
console.log(predict('Research finds promising results in slowing
disease progression'));
// headline
```

You want proof that it's now more accurate? Update the **predict** function to output some values at the start of the function and before the end of the **for** loop:

```
const predict = (data) => {
  console.log(data)
  // ...
    console.log(`${c} => ${p}`)
  }
  return maxClass;
};
```

And the results:

- Unbelievable! This App Predicts Your Past Life Based on Your Habits!
  - clickbait => 0.0012703946815529783
  - headline => 0.0012513993242187493
- Research finds promising results in slowing disease progression
  - clickbait => 0.000016896102540283192
  - headline => 0.027197635964843755

For the first headline the clickbait result is higher. It might not seem like it's higher with 0.00127 verses 0.00125, but as more data is used in training the **probability** values will look more like the second: 0.000016 verses 0.027197. That is the result you're looking for – the words used in the real headline aren't present in many of the clickbait ones, so it's a clear winner there.

You now have a basic classifier for headlines – well done! You could continue to improve this: right now it's comparing individual words but you could make changes to match sequences of words to increase the accuracy even further. Or you could make it support wildcards in the training data so you don't need to support multiple versions of the same sentence and be able to focus on the structure.

Colour classification using supervised machine learning

The client wants a way to categorise various colours into specific groups and, when the user selects their own colour, tells them which group it will belong to. They haven't specified the group names yet, but you know there are a lot of potential colours and determining how they should be grouped together would be too time consuming.

Instead, you've suggested training a machine learning system to categorise some training data into specific groups.

Colours in JavaScript can take many forms, but for this you'll be using hexadecimal values for training, and that's going to be a string that represents the amount of red, green and blue (RGB) to be shown.

```
-   #FF0000 = full red
-   #00FF00 = full green
-   #0000FF = full blue
```

You can't manually determine which colours should be grouped together. Why? Because the hex value of **FF** equals 256. Which means that with 256 potential red, green and blue values results in 16,777,216 colours (256 x 256 x 256). So yeah, make a machine do it.

Let's start with the training data, grouped as red and blue:

```
const trainingData = {
```

```
  red: ['#ff0000', '#ee0000', '#dd0000', '#cc0000', '#bb0000',
'#aa0000'],
  blue: ['#0000ff', '#0000ee', '#0000dd', '#0000cc', '#0000bb',
'#0000aa'],
};
```

You can see how the training data is organised: `red` and `blue` are the labels and various shades of those colours are in an array. Something to remember when working with things like machine learning is that, right now, words like *red* and *blue* have no meaning. Even the hex strings mean nothing so you need to do some extra work to given them the right value to the code you're about to write:

-   The labels need to be converted into something more machine-friendly
-   For each label you need to split those hex strings into their RGB values
-   Each of the RGB values need be used to increase the 'weight' of that value to match the labels
-   Lastly, allow for a new hex string to be entered to get the result

The `red` and `blue` labels could also be called 'classes'. Because a lot of what's about to be written is based on the number of classes it might be a good idea to get the number:

```
const numberOfClasses = Object.keys(trainingData).length;
```

To make the labels more usable to the code they need to be converted into something else. One-Hot encoding is great for working with categories like colours as it's a very simple structure that has a lot of flexibility.

For this red would be transformed into an array value of `[1, 0]` and blue would be transformed into `[0, 1]`. Now for the code:

```
const labelEncoding = Object.keys(trainingData)
  .reduce((acc, label, i, arr) => {
    const oneHot = Array(arr.length).fill(0);
    oneHot[i] = 1;
    acc[label] = oneHot;
    return acc;
  }, {});
```

This takes the keys of the training data and creates a new array with the same number of items, all of which will be **0**. The label's location in the array is then changed to **1**.

Now you have an object that looks like this:

```
{
  blue: [0, 1],
  red: [1, 0]
}
```

Yes, you could have written that yourself, but this will be more valuable soon. Your code will use those arrays when working with the data, which means that if you want a meaningful result then you need a function to take the array and convert it back into a label:

```
const getLabel = (oneHot) => {
  const index = oneHot.indexOf(1);
  return Object.keys(labelEncoding)[index];
};
```

By using the index of the **1** in the **oneHot** array you can find the label in the **labelEncoding** object.

Those hex strings are made of red, green and blue values, and for your code to classify them, or apply a weight to them, then they will need to be split apart. That requires another helper function:

```
const hexToRgb = (hex) => {
  const hexArr = hex.split('');
  return [
    parseInt(hexArr[1] + hexArr[2], 16),
    parseInt(hexArr[3] + hexArr[4], 16),
    parseInt(hexArr[5] + hexArr[6], 16),
  ];
};
```

The RGB values represent 'features' of what your code will classify. If you wanted the code to work with shapes you could classify them by the number of corners they have, vehicles by the number of wheels, countries by GDP, illnesses with symptoms or share prices based on announcements.

The training data you're using is somewhat easy to read for us, but it needs to be transformed into inputs and outputs. This is the data that will be learned, so it needs to be simple:

```javascript
const flatten = (data) => {
  return Object.keys(data).reduce((acc, label) => {
    return acc.concat(
      data[label].map((hexCol) => {
        return {
          input: hexToRgb(hexCol),
          output: label,
        };
      })
    );
  }, []);
};

const trainingSet = flatten(trainingData);
```

The **flatten** function takes your object of data and converts into a linear array of **input/output** objects. It also converts the hex strings into an array of RGB colour values.

```javascript
[{
  input: [255, 0, 0],
  output: "red"
}, {
  input: [238, 0, 0],
  output: "red"
}, ... ]
```

Everything done so far has been to create the **trainingSet** array: this is the actual data that will be 'learned'. Next thing that needs to happen is for the inputs and labels to be extracted:

```javascript
const inputs = [];
const labels = [];
```

```
for (let pair of trainingSet) {
  inputs.push(pair.input);
  const oneHot = labelEncoding[pair.output];
  labels.push(oneHot);
}
```

Now two new arrays, **inputs** and **labels**, have been created. In another iteration you could simplify that and refactor the flatten function to handle this without the extra step, but for now this is fine.

For each class (or colour) there needs to be a weight given to each of the RGB values. What those values are right now doesn't matter because they will change as the code learns. You can use the number of classes to fill an array with random values:

```
const weights = Array(numberOfClasses).fill().map(
  () => [Math.random(), Math.random(), Math.random()]
);
```

Similar thing for the biases but they're just for each class:

```
const bias = Array(numberOfClasses).fill().map(
  () => Math.random()
);
```

Now you need a function to predict the class based on the RGB input. Right now you have two classes, red and blue, so for each class you need:

- R x current classes' R weight, plus
- G x current classes' G weight, plus
- B x current classes' G weight, plus
- current classes' bias

Which looks like this:

```
const predict = ([r, g, b]) => {
  const sum = Object.keys(labelEncoding).map((_, i) => {
    return (
      r * weights[i][0] +
```

```
      g * weights[i][1] +
      b * weights[i][2] +
      bias[i]
   );
 });

 const index = sum.indexOf(Math.max(...sum));
 return Object.values(labelEncoding)[index];
};
```

The **index** of the maximum **sum** will return the one-hot encoded label. In the first few predictions this will make no sense, but as it learns and has the same data reinforce the weights your code will begin to make more meaningful predictions.

- The weights and biases have been seeded with random values, but for now let's use **0.1**
- Start with full red: **[255, 0, 0]**:
   o For the Red class **[1, 0]**:
      ▪ 255 x 0.1 + 0 x 0.1 + 0 x 0.1 + 0.1
      ▪ 25.6
   o For the Blue class **[0, 1]**:
      ▪ 0 x 0.1 + 0 x 0.1 + 0 x 0.1 + 0.1
      ▪ 0.1
   o This returns an array of **[26.1, 0.1]**
- The maximum sum is 26.1 and the index of the maximum sum is 0 so it returns the Red classes' one-hot encoded label

The weights and biases will change as it receives more data and learns. Which is where this loop comes in to make the learning happen:

```
const learningRate = 0.01;

for (let i = 0; i < 1000; i++) {
  for (let j = 0; j < inputs.length; j++) {
    const prediction = predict(inputs[j]);

    const error = labels[j].map(
      (label, index) => label - prediction[index]
```

```
  );

  for (let k = 0; k < weights.length; k++) {
    weights[k] = weights[k].map(
      (weight, l) => weight + error[k] *
                      inputs[j][l] * learningRate
    );
    bias[k] += error[k] * learningRate;
  }
 }
}
```

The learning rate (0.01) and the number of epochs (1,000), are values you can change but for now they're fine for testing. If you want to use `console.log` to view some of the values it's *strongly* recommended you reduce the number of epochs to a much smaller value.

Every time the training data is used (`inputs`) the result of the prediction is used to reinforce the weights and biases while also taking into account any errors. The combined errors and learning rate change the bias to improve the accuracy.

Now to see it work:

```
const predictFromInput = (input) => {
  const rgb = hexToRgb(input.toLowerCase());
  const oneHot = predict(rgb);
  return getLabel(oneHot);
};

console.log('#FF0000', predictFromInput('#FF0000'));
console.log('#0000FF', predictFromInput('#0000FF'));
console.log('#110000', predictFromInput('#110000'));
console.log('#000011', predictFromInput('#000011'));
```

The `predictFromInput` function takes the hex string and tries to predict the class/colour. The first two tests use the full red and blue to check to make sure it works:

```
'#FF0000', 'red'
'#0000FF', 'blue'
```

The next two tests show the power of training: you never used **#110000** or **#000011** in the training data but it accurately classified them.

```
'#110000', 'red'
'#000011', 'blue'
```

Of course, if you give it something it hasn't been trained on it will give you an incorrect result:

```
console.log('#00FF00', predictFromInput('#00FF00'));
```

It only knows red and blue, so you can't expect it to suddenly know what green is. Fortunately, the training data can be easily updated:

```
const trainingData = {
  red: [...],
  green: ['#00ff00', '#00ee00', '#00dd00', '#00cc00', '#00bb00',
'#00aa00'],
  blue: [...]
};
```

Now that it knows what green is…

```
predictFromInput('#FF0000'); // red
predictFromInput('#00FF00'); // green
predictFromInput('#0000FF'); // blue
predictFromInput('#110000'); // red
predictFromInput('#001100'); // green
predictFromInput('#000011'); // blue
```

Yellow might be a challenge as it represents a combination of red and green. Updating the training data is just as easy as it was for green, and nothing in the rest of your code has to change.

```
const trainingData = {
  ...
  yellow: ['#ffff00', '#eeee00', '#dddd00', '#cccc00', '#bbbb00',
'#aaaa00']
```

```
};
```

```
console.log('#FFFF00', predictFromInput('#FFFF00'));
// yellow


console.log('#EEFF00', predictFromInput('#EEFF00'));
// yellow


console.log('#FF1100', predictFromInput('#FF1100'));
// red
```

Seems like the flexibility you added earlier has paid off. Keep in mind that every additional class requires more processing during the training.

That was a very complex exercise but if you're seeing similar results then you've done really well! And if you're wondering: you used a perceptron model – or supervised learning – where the training data you gave the code already had a label.

Machine learning is complex. As humans we take the ability to learn new things for granted and writing code that can learn is a *massive* undertaking. If you want to take this kind of learning further it would be good to search for third-party libraries that can handle the heavy lifting.

Charting

Seeing is believing, and that also applies to data. Things like linear regression and trendlines sound great but at some point, you want to see the results. That's why your client wants you to build a chart. There are a few steps that need to be done:

- X and Y axis
  - Min and max numbers to show
  - Length
  - Ticks
- Showing the data

Unfortunately, this exercise is not a Node-friendly one: browsers only from this point. To make this project easier to manage it would be a good idea for it to be done using a class. Start with the **constructor**:

```
class Chart {
  constructor(selector, data, options) {
    this.el = document.querySelector(selector);
```

This **constructor** accepts three arguments: the **selector** that'll be used to find the element to act as the parent that contains your chart, the **data** the chart needs to show, and some **options** to help customise it (like padding and intervals).

If you're making this for others it might be a good idea to check that the parent element actually exists, and that it's the right kind of element:

```
    if (!this.el) {
        throw new Error(`No element found matching selector
${selector}`);
    }
    if (this.el.tagName !== 'DIV') {
        throw new Error(`Element with selector ${selector} must be
a div`);
    }
```

Now that you're sure the element is the one you want, you should create the SVG element that will hold the chart:

```
    this.svg = document.createElementNS(
        'http://www.w3.org/2000/svg', 'svg'
    );
    this.svg.setAttribute('width', this.el.width);
    this.svg.setAttribute('height', this.el.height);
    this.svg.style.border = '1px solid black';
    this.el.appendChild(this.svg);

    this.options = options;
    this.data = data;
    }
}
```

Scalable Vector Graphics (SVG) will be used to draw the chart so the first thing the **constructor** needs to do it create one. The **document.createElementNS** is where this happens, and then you can set different attributes before appending it to the parent **element**.

You've started the class, but you'll need to initialise it so you can see some data. How about you reuse the values from the linear regression project as the **data**:

```
const data = [
    {
        name: 'Series 1',
        colour: 'red',
        values: [
```

```
      { x: 0, y: 1 },
      { x: 1, y: 2 },
      { x: 2, y: 3 },
      { x: 13, y: 4 },
      { x: 14, y: 5 },
    ],
  }
];
```

The next part involves creating the **div** to be the parent element that wraps around the chart. If you prefer to use HTML then:

```
<div id="chart" width="400" height="300"></div>
```

Or you can use JavaScript to create it:

```
const chartEl = document.createElement('div');
chartEl.width = 400;
chartEl.height = 300;
chartEl.id = 'chart';
document.body.appendChild(chartEl);
```

You might have noticed the **createElement** used here and **createElementNS** used for the SVG: **createElementNS** allows you to add a namespace (NS) to the element – the **http://www.w3.org/2000/svg** - and for SVG that's required.

To initialise the chart class:

```
const chart = new Chart('#chart', data, {
  x: {
    padding: 10,
    labelGap: 20,
    interval: 1
  },
  y: {
    padding: 10,
    labelGap: 10,
    interval: 1
  }
```

```
});
```

Great! That's created the **div** to hold the chart and given it the **data** and **options** it will need. Time to go back to the class. At the end of the **constructor** you need to call a method to make it draw:

```
this.data = data;

this.draw(); // <- new
}
```

There are several methods needed for this class:

- A main draw method that will be used to prepare and ultimately draw the chart
- Another to draw the X and Y axis
- The method to draw the data on the chart
- A very important method to clear the chart
- One to find the limits of the data
- A method to figure out what ticks for each axis are needed
- And finally, a way to update the data

You can add them to your class (you'll need the **draw** one ASAP as your class calls it in the **constructor**, but you can keep it empty for now):

```
draw() {}

drawAxis() {}

drawData(axis, limits, xAxisLength, yAxisLength) {}

clear() {}

getLimits() {}

getTicks(limits) {}

update(data) {}
```

Starting from the bottom is the **update** method that accepts new **data**:

```
update(data) {
  this.data = data;
  this.draw();
}
```

The new **data** will replace the values already in the class's scope (**this.data**) before calling the **draw** method again. You *could* destroy the chart and then re-initialise it with new data, but that's more work than necessary. That being said, you do need a way to clear the SVG to make sure you're working with a clean slate:

```
clear() {
  const { svg } = this;
  while (svg.firstChild) {
    svg.removeChild(svg.firstChild);
  }
}
```

This loops through the child elements of the SVG and removes them (as long as there are elements to remove).

Right now, you have the data but to visualise it with a chart you need to know it's limits – it's minimum and maximum x and y values. Your **data** variable is an array that currently has one set of **values**, but to make future-proofing a bit easier you should allow it to support multiple data sets.

With that in mind:

```
getLimits() {
  const limits = {
    xMin: 0, xMax: 0,
    yMin: 0, yMax: 0
  };
  this.data.forEach((series) => {
    const xValues = series.values
      .map((value) => value.x);
    const yValues = series.values
      .map((value) => value.y);
    limits.xMin = Math.min(limits.xMin, ...xValues);
```

```
    limits.xMax = Math.max(limits.xMax, ...xValues);
    limits.yMin = Math.min(limits.yMin, ...yValues);
    limits.yMax = Math.max(limits.yMax, ...yValues);
  });
  return limits;
}
```

Once you have all the x and y values you can determine the min and max limits for each axis. Now that you have the **limits** you can start working on the ticks – the small markers on each axis that show a label

```
getTicks(limits) {
  const { xMin, xMax, yMin, yMax } = limits;
  const { x, y } = this.options;
  const tickLabelsX = [];
  const tickLabelsY = [];
  let tickX = xMin;
  let tickY = yMin;
  while (tickX <= xMax) {
    tickLabelsX.push(tickX);
    tickX += x.interval;
  }
  while (tickY <= yMax) {
    tickLabelsY.push(tickY);
    tickY += y.interval;
  }
  return { tickLabelsX, tickLabelsY };
}
```

The **interval** you set in your chart's **options** are used here: basically you keep adding ticks until you hit the maximum for that axis, and the **interval** determines how many numbers to skep between each **tick**.

And now for the heavy lifting: drawing each axis:

```
drawAxis() {
  const limits = this.getLimits();
  const { tickLabelsX, tickLabelsY } = this.getTicks(limits);
```

You just created the **getLimits** and **getTicks** methods, and this is where it gets complicated. The advantage of working with SVG is that JavaScript gives you the ability to measure the size of elements, which is great because you need to know the width of the labels on the y axis to push the axis away from the edge and not cut the labels. The problem is that you need to create the labels before you can get their size.

Let's start small:

```
let maxXAxisLabelHeight = 0;
let maxYAxisLabelWidth = 0;
const tickLabels = {
```

The **tickLabels** object will be used to reference the labels after they're created: that way they can be repositioned once the final calculations are complete. The ticks on the x axis go left to right:

```
const tickLabels = {
  x: tickLabelsX.map((tick) => {
    const tickLabel = document.createElementNS(
      'http://www.w3.org/2000/svg',
      'text'
    );
    tickLabel.setAttribute('text-anchor', 'middle');
    tickLabel.textContent = tick;
    this.svg.appendChild(tickLabel);
    maxXAxisLabelHeight = Math.max(
      maxXAxisLabelHeight,
      tickLabel.getBBox().height
    );
    return tickLabel;
  }),
```

For each **tick** you need to create a text element for the SVG, set its **textContent**, append it to the SVG element, determine if its height is the largest and then return the **tickLabel** it so you can use it later. The y axis ticks are similar:

```
  y: tickLabelsY.map((tick) => {
    const tickLabel = document.createElementNS(
```

241

```
      'http://www.w3.org/2000/svg',
      'text'
    );
    tickLabel.setAttribute('text-anchor', 'end');
    tickLabel.setAttribute('alignment-baseline', 'middle');
    tickLabel.textContent = tick;
    this.svg.appendChild(tickLabel);
    maxYAxisLabelWidth = Math.max(
      maxYAxisLabelWidth,
      tickLabel.getBBox().width
    );
    return tickLabel;
  })
```

This is necessary because the width of a label like 0 will be less than the width of 100, or 1,000,000. Once you know the maximum sizes needed to show the tick labels you can use that to push each axis away from the edge to give it enough room. This is how that happens:

```
const axis = {
  x1: this.options.x.padding +
    maxYAxisLabelWidth +
    this.options.y.labelGap,
  x2: this.el.width - this.options.x.padding -
    this.options.y.labelGap,
  y1: this.options.y.padding +
    this.options.x.labelGap / 2,
  y2: this.el.height -
    this.options.y.padding -
    maxXAxisLabelHeight -
    this.options.x.labelGap / 2
};
```

Looking at the maths here might make you question what's going on. For things like charts when the y value increases it goes up, but that's the reverse in SVG:

- Chart: X = 0, Y = 0 – bottom left

- SVG: X = 0, Y = 0 – top left

So:

- **x1** – left: padding + y axis label width + y label gap
- **x2** – right: width – padding – y label gap
- **y1** – top: padding + x label gap
- **y2** – bottom: height – padding – x axis label height – x label gap

Because you went to the effort of determining the x/y start/end values, calculating the length of each axis is pretty easy:

```
const xAxisLength = axis.x2 - axis.x1;
const yAxisLength = axis.y2 - axis.y1;
```

Time to see some results! Draw the two lines needed for the x and y axis:

```
const xAxis = document.createElementNS(
    'http://www.w3.org/2000/svg',
    'line'
);
xAxis.setAttribute('x1', axis.x1);
xAxis.setAttribute('y1', axis.y2);
xAxis.setAttribute('x2', axis.x2);
xAxis.setAttribute('y2', axis.y2);
xAxis.setAttribute('stroke', 'black');
this.svg.appendChild(xAxis);

const yAxis = document.createElementNS(
    'http://www.w3.org/2000/svg',
    'line'
);
yAxis.setAttribute('x1', axis.x1);
yAxis.setAttribute('y1', axis.y1);
yAxis.setAttribute('x2', axis.x1);
yAxis.setAttribute('y2', axis.y2);
yAxis.setAttribute('stroke', 'black');
this.svg.appendChild(yAxis);
```

And then go update your **draw** method so you can see what you've achieved:

```
draw() {
  this.clear();
  this.drawAxis();
}
```

You should see this:

Go on, congratulate yourself. It was *a lot* of effort to get this far, but you can now begin to see what you're working towards.

Those lengths are also needed to draw each tick: if you have to draw 5 ticks you need to work with percentages – for example, your x axis has a length of 200:

Tick	Percent	Result
1	1 / 5 ticks = 0.2 = 20%	20% of 200 = 40px
2	2 / 5 ticks = 0.4 = 40%	40% of 200 = 80px
3	3/ 5 ticks = 0.6 = 60%	60% of 200 = 120px

| 4 | 4 /5 ticks = 0.8 = 80% | 80% of 200 = 160px |
| 5 | 5 / 5 ticks = 1 = 100% | 100% of 200 = 200px |

```
tickLabelsX.forEach((tick) => {
  const tickLine = document.createElementNS(
    'http://www.w3.org/2000/svg',
    'line'
  );
  const tickX = axis.x1 + (tick / limits.xMax) * xAxisLength;
  tickLine.setAttribute('x1', tickX);
  tickLine.setAttribute('y1', axis.y2);
  tickLine.setAttribute('x2', tickX);
  tickLine.setAttribute('y2', axis.y2 + 5);
  tickLine.setAttribute('stroke', 'black');
  this.svg.appendChild(tickLine);
});
```

The **tickX** variable allows you to reuse the x value and draw a 5px vertical line where each **tick** should be and append it to the SVG. It's a similar process for the ticks in the y axis:

```
tickLabelsY.forEach((tick) => {
  const tickLine = document.createElementNS(
    'http://www.w3.org/2000/svg',
    'line'
  );
  const tickY = axis.y2 - (tick / limits.yMax) * yAxisLength;
  tickLine.setAttribute('x1', axis.x1);
  tickLine.setAttribute('y1', tickY);
  tickLine.setAttribute('x2', axis.x1 - 5);
  tickLine.setAttribute('y2', tickY);
  tickLine.setAttribute('stroke', 'black');
  this.svg.appendChild(tickLine);
});
```

Check your progress:

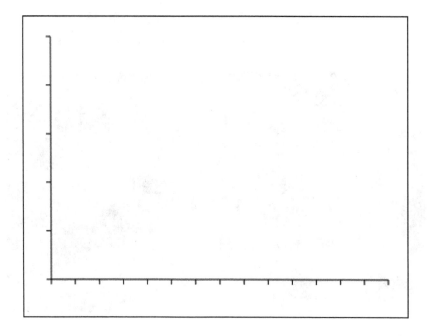

The ticks are showing up correctly. Very nice! The only thing missing from each axis are the labels. Remember earlier when they were created to get their measurements? They're still there but you can't see them because they don't have a position. Time to give them a new home:

```
tickLabels.x.forEach((tickLabel, i) => {
    tickLabel.setAttribute(
      'x',
      axis.x1 + (tickLabelsX[i] / limits.xMax) * xAxisLength
    );
    tickLabel.setAttribute('y', axis.y2 +
this.options.x.labelGap);
    });


    tickLabels.y.forEach((tickLabel, i) => {
      tickLabel.setAttribute('x', axis.x1 -
this.options.y.labelGap);
      tickLabel.setAttribute(
        'y',
        axis.y2 - (tickLabelsY[i] / limits.yMax) * yAxisLength
```

```
    );
  });
```

And...

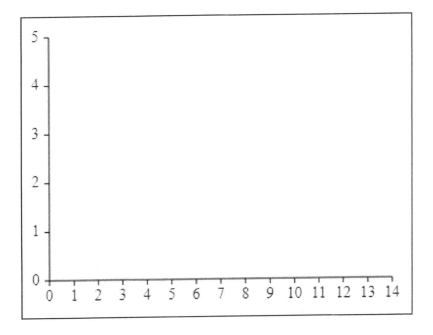

Well done! The x and y axis are complete and you're nearly ready to draw the data. Several of those calculations you did will be needed to show the data so they're worth returning:

```
return {
  axis,
  limits,
  xAxisLength,
  yAxisLength,
};
}
```

And after making a final change to your **draw** method, it's time to show the data.

```
draw() {
  this.clear();
  const {
    axis,
    limits,
    xAxisLength,
    yAxisLength
  } = this.drawAxis();
  this.drawData(
    axis, limits, xAxisLength, yAxisLength
  );
}
```

By returning the `axis`, `limits`, `xAxisLength` and `yAxisLength` you can use them when drawing the data to correctly position each dot. Speaking of drawing data:

```
drawData(axis, limits, xAxisLength, yAxisLength) {
  this.data.forEach((series) => {
    series.values.forEach((value) => {
      const dot = document.createElementNS(
        'http://www.w3.org/2000/svg',
        'circle'
      );
      dot.setAttribute('cx', axis.x1 + (value.x / limits.xMax)
* xAxisLength);
      dot.setAttribute('cy', axis.y2 - (value.y / limits.yMax)
* yAxisLength);
      dot.setAttribute('r', 5);
      dot.setAttribute('fill', series.colour);
      this.svg.appendChild(dot);
    });
  });
}
```

Each **dot** is an SVG circle with a radius of five pixels positioned according to their x and y values. You should now have a chart that looks like this:

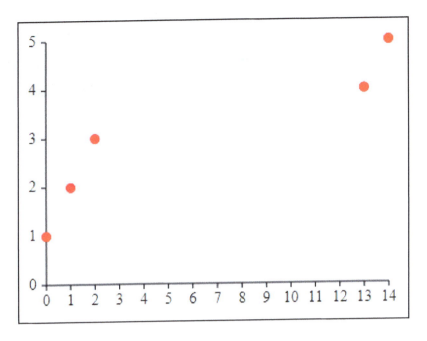

That's it – you did it! You successfully created a chart using an SVG that you can now use to show your data. How about some exponential growth:

```
const data = [
  {
    name: 'Check',
    colour: 'green',
    values: [
      { x: 1, y: 1 },
      { x: 2, y: 2 },
      { x: 3, y: 4 },
      { x: 4, y: 8 },
      { x: 5, y: 16 },
    ]
  }
];
```

And a quick change to the **options**:

```
y: {
  padding: 10,
  labelGap: 10,
  interval: 3
}
```

This will give you green dots:

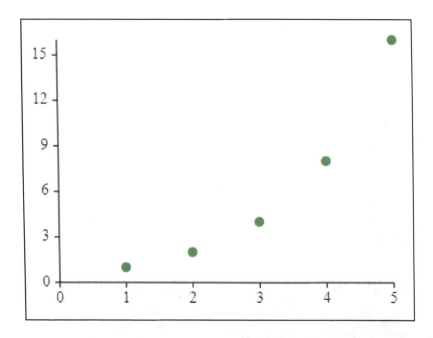

But what about some of those other methods, like **update**? You can wrap it in a timer so that that you can see the data change:

```
setTimeout(() => {
  chart.update([
    {
      name: 'Series 1',
      colour: '#bada55',
      values: Array(5)
        .fill()
        .map((_, i) => (
          { x: i * 10, y: Math.pow(i, 2) }
        ))
```

```
    }
 ]);
}, 2000);
```

After two seconds the chart should update itself!

Inspirational NFTs

NFTs, or non-fungible tokens, is something your client has read about and is interested in pursuing. They need you to generate the 'artwork' that will be used with these tokens. But given how many offerings there are with NFTs you need to find a way to differentiate your work from others. You've suggested adding inspirational quotes to the images.

Here's your plan:

- Generate a pattern based on a seed (like the token itself?)
- Add a quote
- Make it downloadable
- Profit!

This uses the **canvas** element, so it's necessary to also have a HTML page:

```
<!DOCTYPE html>
<html>
<head>
  <title>NFTs</title>
</head>
<body>
  <canvas id="canvas" width="500" height="500"></canvas>

  <button id="download">Download</button>
```

```
<script src="./canvas-text.js"></script>
</html>
```

And just like before:

```
const canvas = document.getElementById('canvas');
const ctx = canvas.getContext('2d');

const width = canvas.width;
const height = canvas.height;
```

You need to get the 2d context so you can do your drawing. To make sure you've set everything up correctly it would be a good idea to add some colour:

```
ctx.fillStyle = '#bada55';
ctx.fillRect(10, 10, width - 20, height - 20);
```

This fills the **canvas** with a solid colour but keeps a **10px** wide border. You can change that if you prefer. Next you need a seed:

```
const seed = '3cb5';
```

In reality this would be longer, but the **seed** will control various parts of the drawing. For this exercise you'll be drawing a simple grid background that fills various circles depending on the values in the seed.

```
const size = 10;
const radius = 4;
```

The **size** is for the width and height of the grid's columns and rows, while the **radius** is for the circles.

```
const rows = height / size;
const columns = width / size;
```

Using the size and canvas dimensions you can determine how many rows and columns need to be drawn:

```
ctx.strokeStyle = '#fff';
```

```
for (let c = 0; c < columns; c++) {
  for (let r = 0; r < rows; r++) {
    ctx.beginPath();
    ctx.ellipse(
      c * size, r * size, radius, radius, 0, 0, 2 * Math.PI
    );
    ctx.stroke();
  }
}
```

For each column (and then each row) a circle with the radius is drawn. Here's what it looks like so far:

Your **seed** has two numbers in it. Get them:

```
const xVal = parseInt(seed.charAt(0));
const yVal = parseInt(seed.charAt(3));
```

You can now make some changes to the circles to fill them depending on whether or not the rows or columns are divisible by the **xVal** and **yVal** numbers:

```
ctx.strokeStyle = '#fff';
```

```
for (let c = 0; c < columns; c++) {
  for (let r = 0; r < rows; r++) {
    if (r % xVal === 0 || c % yVal === 0) { // <- new
      ctx.fillStyle = '#fff';
    } else {
      ctx.fillStyle = 'transparent';
    } // <- new
    ctx.beginPath();
    ctx.ellipse(
      c * size, r * size, radius, radius, 0, 0, 2 * Math.PI
    );
    ctx.fill(); // <- new
    ctx.stroke();
  }
}
```

Last thing to do is to add an inspirational quote:

```
ctx.fillStyle = '#000';
ctx.font = '48px sans-serif';
const text = 'Just stick with it. What seems so hard now will one
day be your warm up.';
ctx.fillText(text, 10, 50);
```

You've set the fill style, font and added the text:

And there's a problem. When adding text to the `canvas` it doesn't wrap when it reaches the end. This is not ideal. In the past, you had to create a temporary HTML element with the same text, font and other formatting before playing around with the words to figure out when they should break so they could flow onto multiple lines before added them to the `canvas`.

This can now be done entirely in the `canvas` with the `measureText` method:

```
const wrapText = (context, text, maxWidth) => {
  const words = text.split(' ');
  const lines = [];
  let line = '';
```

The `text` argument is `split` so you can measure each word. As long at the font information has been set the `measureText` method will be able to give you the correct metrics (width, height, all that) without having to render anything.

```
words.forEach((word, i) => {
  const testLine = `${line}${word} `;
  const metrics = context.measureText(testLine);
  const testWidth = metrics.width;
```

```
  if (testWidth > maxWidth && i > 0) {
    lines.push(line);
    line = `${word} `;
  } else {
    line = testLine;
  }
});

lines.push(line);
return lines;
};
```

On every **word** it measures the **width** of the current **line**. If that **line** is more than the **maxWidth** then the current **line** (without the new word) is pushed into the **lines** array, otherwise it adds it to the current **line**.

As an example, if the current **word** is 'seems':

- current line = '**Just stick with it. What** '
- line + new word = '**Just stick with it. What seems** '
- if **measureText**'s returned **width** is more than **maxWidth**:
  - add '**Just stick with it. What** ' to the **lines** array
  - set **line** to '**seems** '
- else
  - line = '**Just stick with it. What seems** '

The **lines.push(line)** is necessary to pick up any remaining words. Now that the **wrapText** function tells you where to break the text, you can add it to the canvas:

```
ctx.font = '48px sans-serif';
ctx.fillStyle = '#000';
ctx.textBaseline = 'middle';
ctx.textAlign = 'center';
const lineHeight = 54;
```

It's very important to set the font details *before* you call the **wrapText** function.

```
const text = 'Just stick with it. What seems so hard now will one
day be your warm up.';
const multilineText = wrapText(ctx, text, 400);
```

The **multilineText** array now has the correct line-breaking. To add
the text:

```
const yOffset = (height / 2) -
                (multilineText.length * lineHeight) / 2;
multilineText.forEach((line, i) => {
  ctx.fillText(
    line, width / 2, yOffset + i * lineHeight
  );
});
```

That **yOffset** will be used to ensure the text is vertically aligned. Here's
what you should see:

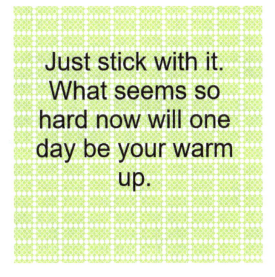

No more alignment or wrapping issues! But don't stop here: you can
determine the colours, fonts, shapes and other properties of the generated
image by using the **seed**:

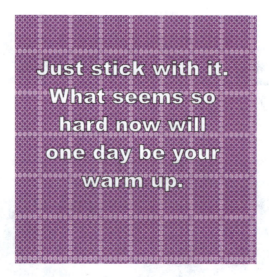

Do you see how the change in font allowed the **wrapText** function to maintain the wrapping?

Adding more background shapes, colours, blend modes, font options and a variety of quotes will enable you to generate a huge number of images. Of course, you'll want people to download the images (they only own the **seed** after-all):

```
const downloadBtn = document.getElementById('download');
downloadBtn.addEventListener('click', () => {
  const dataURL = canvas.toDataURL('image/png');
  window.open(dataURL);
});
```

This enables the **canvas** to be converted into an image: ready to be saved and used in other ways. The URL opens in a new browser tab/window and what your customer's do next with the image is up to them.

Mandelbrot Set

Your client has asked for a Mandlebrot background for a poster. The Mandelbrot Set is a fractal: a geometric shape that repeats itself. It's not like a typical pattern – the more you zoom into a fractal the more detail it shows – and that detail is more of itself.

This type of fractal uses something called Complex numbers: a combination of *real* and *imaginary* numbers. If you want a visual then real numbers are something you would see on the x-axis of a graph (left-and-right), while imaginary numbers would be on the y-axis (up-and-down).

Depending on which part of the set you're looking at it can show different things, and the client wants to see some examples before a larger version is made. Some HTML is needed to make this work:

```html
<!DOCTYPE html>
<html>
  <head>
    <title>Mandelbrot</title>
  </head>
  <body>
    <canvas id="canvas" width="800" height="500"></canvas>
    <script src="./mandelbrot.js"></script>
  </body>
</html>
```

Now that there's a **canvas** element to use, you need to access it with

JavaScript:

```
const canvas = document.getElementById('canvas');
const ctx = canvas.getContext('2d');
```

The `ctx` is the drawable part of the `canvas` element. You used it previously for Browser Fingerprinting to measure text with different fonts, but this time you'll be using it to draw.

```
const width = canvas.width;
const height = canvas.height;
```

The `width` and `height` are defined in the HTML, but they're needed in your code too. If you change the attributes there then that will change these values so you won't have to define them twice.

This next part might annoy some mathematicians, but for the sake of simplicity:

```
const xAxis = { start: -2, end: 1 };
const yAxis = { start: -1, end: 1 };
```

These are *supposed* to represent the start and end of the real (`xAxis`) and imaginary (`yAxis`) numbers. It's better to think of these as the limits of what you're drawing. They have no relation to the size of the `canvas`, and you can use them to focus on other areas of the fractal.

You're going to want some colour on this fractal, and instead of picking them yourself you can generate them:

```
const colours = Array(16).fill().map(() => {
  const r = Math.floor(Math.random() * 255);
  const g = Math.floor(Math.random() * 255);
  const b = Math.floor(Math.random() * 255);
  return `rgb(${r}, ${g}, ${b})`;
});
```

The `colours` array will now be filled with 16 randomly generated values. The repetition in the code is not ideal and you could convert the `Math.floor(Math.random() * 255)` into a function, but for now this is okay. You could also define these yourself in the array: it could be any number of colours.

Before starting the Mandelbrot generator function you should check to make sure the **canvas** can be drawn on:

```
const draw = () => {
  ctx.fillStyle = colours[0];
  ctx.fillRect(0, 0, width, height);
};
draw();
```

You should see a block of colour being drawn to your **canvas**. The basic setup is done! As for what's drawn…

Mandelbrot Sets are drawn using *a lot* of maths:

```
const mandelbrot = (c) => {
  const maxCount = 80;
  let iteration = 0;
  let z = { x: 0, y: 0 };
  let p = { x: 0, y: 0 };
```

This will check if the complex number (**c**) is in the Mandelbrot Set. It starts with **z = 0** and iterates until the right conditions are met in the loop you're about to write.

The **maxCount** and **iteration** will determine how much detail to render. Because you're working with pixels there's only so much detail you can show so the count doesn't have to be that high.

The **z** and **p** variables are complex numbers but again for the sake of simplicity they'll use **x** and **y** properties.

```
let distance = 0;
while (distance <= 2 && iteration < maxCount) {
  p = {
    x: Math.pow(z.x, 2) - Math.pow(z.y, 2),
    y: 2 * z.x * z.y,
  };
  z = {
    x: p.x + c.x,
    y: p.y + c.y,
  };
```

While the **distance** is less than or equal to 2 and the number of **iterations** is less than the **maxCount**:

- **p.x** needs to be calculated, which is the difference of the squared **z.x** and **z.y** values,
- **p.y** also needs to be calculated, which is the **z.x** and **z.y** values multiplied by 2.

Calculating the **p** values are just an interim step: it's the **z** values that matter (but more on that later).

```
distance = Math.sqrt(Math.pow(z.x, 2) + Math.pow(z.y, 2));
++iteration;
}
```

The **distance** is calculated using a modified version of the Pythagorean Theorem (the difference between the first and second points are the width and height):

$$distance = \sqrt{width^2 + height^2}$$

```
return {
  iteration,
  isMandelbrotSet: distance <= 2
};
};
```

Now update the **draw** function, and you can remove what was previously there:

```
const draw = () => {
  const xAxisWidth = xAxis.end - xAxis.start;
  const yAxisHeight = yAxis.end - yAxis.start;
  const c = { x: 0, y: 0 };

  for (let i = 0; i < width; i++) {
    for (let j = 0; j < height; j++) {
      c.x = xAxis.start + (i / width) * xAxisWidth;
      c.y = yAxis.start + (j / height) * yAxisHeight;
```

The **c** is a scaled value of the current pixel on your **canvas**. It will be between the **xAxis** and **yAxis** values declared earlier. When that is passed to the **mandelbrot** function it will determine if it's part of the set:

```
const { iteration, isMandelbrotSet } = mandelbrot(c);
ctx.fillStyle = isMandelbrotSet
  ? '#000'
  : colours[iteration % colours.length];
ctx.fillRect(i, j, 1, 1);
}
}
};
```

A value that is in the set will be coloured with **#000** while those not in the set will be assigned a colour from the **colours** array based on how many iterations it went through before it found the result.

You should now see something like this (your colours will be different):

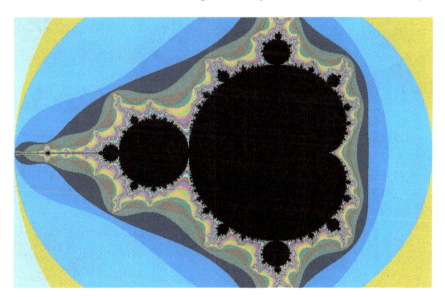

You can also add some more code to zoom in and out:

```
const zoom = (e) => {
  const { target, offsetX: x, offsetY: y } = e;
  const scale = e.shiftKey ? 2 : 0.5;

  const xAxisWidth = xAxis.end - xAxis.start;
  const yAxisHeight = yAxis.end - yAxis.start;

  const newWidth = xAxisWidth * scale;
  const newHeight = yAxisHeight * scale;

  xAxis.start = xAxis.start + (x / target.width)
              * xAxisWidth - newWidth / 2;
  xAxis.end = xAxis.start + (x / target.width)
              * xAxisWidth + newWidth / 2;
  yAxis.start = yAxis.start + (y / target.height)
              * yAxisHeight - newHeight / 2;
  yAxis.end = yAxis.start + (y / target.height)
              * yAxisHeight + newHeight / 2;
  console.log(xAxis, yAxis);
  draw();
};

canvas.addEventListener('click', zoom);
```

This will enable you to change the range used on the xAxis and yAxis values. It will also give you the new values so you can record them for later. The scale changes based on whether or not you hold down the shift key while you click.

Zoom in to get yourself some special shots:

Remember that it's JavaScript so you can't go into infinity because of the limitations of the numbers used, but you can still zoom in quite a distance to see some different things.

If you want an explanation – the `while` loop with the `p` and `z` values is where the magic happens. When the scaled pixel (`c`) is passed to the `mandelbrot` function it's used to determine if it's within the set.

The initial `z` value is 0,0. In every iteration of the loop a new point (`p`) is calculated and the `z` value is updated. If the `distance` between the `z` value and the origin is more than 2 then it's not part of the Mandelbrot Set, and those are the coloured pixels you see in the image. Only the black pixels are in the set (you could give them another colour).

That loop is necessary because you need to keep testing to see if the `z` value remains close to the origin. It's following this equation:

$$Z_{n+1} = Z_n{}^2 + C$$

The next `z` value is calculated from the current one being squared and then having the `c` (the scaled current pixel) added to it. Each iteration could increase the `distance` to the point where it's no longer part of the set, so changing the `maxCount` will give different results:

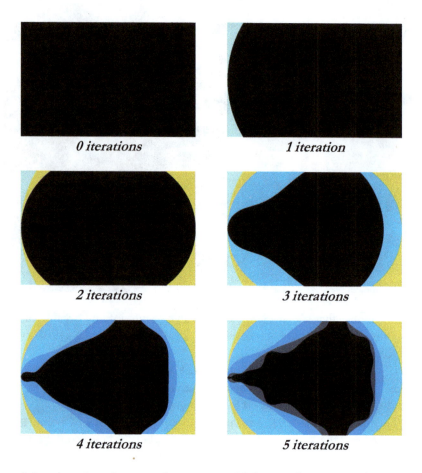

0 iterations   *1 iteration*

2 iterations   *3 iterations*

4 iterations   *5 iterations*

More iterations increase the accuracy. If the xAxis and yAxis remain the same then it's likely all of the pixels in along the center of the canvas will be in the Mandelbrot Set, and those in the corners won't be.

You have your poster's background generator. And you don't have to stop there: you could render multiple sets on top of each other using different parameters and colours to create entirely unique images. This could even replace the pattern generator used in the previous NFT project.

Plague simulation

Time to bring back those memories of home quarantine, wearing masks, gloves and other protective gear – you've been asked to simulate a plague. The idea is to show how infection spreads from one person to others based on distance and how infectious the disease is. For this there's some initial information you can work with:

- r0: the number of people who could be infected
- chance of survival
- the minimum distance the infection can't go beyond
- and the simulated population in the space

This simulation will use the `canvas` element – because you want it animated – so it will need some HTML elements:

```
<!DOCTYPE html>
<html>
  <head>
    <title>Plague Sim</title>
  </head>
  <body>
    <canvas id="canvas" width="500" height="500"></canvas>
    <script src="./plague-sim.js"></script>
  </body>
</html>
```

To visualise the people you need for them to be a little self-reliant in how the data is handled, like whether they're infected, alive and their current health, so a class would be effective:

```
class Person {
  constructor(x, y) {
    this.alive = true;
    this.infected = false;
    this.daysInfected = 0;
    this.isImmune = false;
    this.health = 100;
    this.x = x;
    this.y = y;
  }
```

When a person is created the only information you need to pass to the constructor are their x and y values for the canvas. Everything else can happily use the defaults. Now for a method to infect the person:

```
infect() {
  this.infected = true;
}
```

Nice and simple. And the last thing for the class is a way to manage the person's health:

```
update() {
  if (this.infected && this.alive) {
    this.daysInfected++;
    this.health -= 10;

    if (this.health <= 0 || Math.random() > chanceSurvival) {
      this.alive = false;
    }

    if (this.daysInfected > 7) {
      this.infected = false;
      this.isImmune = true;
```

```
      }
    }
  }
}
```

When the **update** method is called it checks to see if the person is both infected and alive. If they are their **daysInfected** in increased and their **health** declines. The **chanceSurvival** hasn't been declared yet, so here it is:

```
const r0 = 2;
const chanceSurvival = 0.99;
const minDistance = 20;
const population = 1000;
```

Usually you can't use a variable until *after* it's been declared, and if the class is in the same file as the rest of the code then that remains true – you haven't created the person using the class *yet*, so it's not a significant problem. If you wanted the class to be another file then you would include **chanceSurvival** as an argument in the constructor:

```
constructor(x, y, chanceSurvival) {
   this.chanceSurvival = chanceSurvival;
```

And then update the class to use the new local value:

```
      if (this.health <= 0 || Math.random() >
this.chanceSurvival) {
```

Now for the **canvas** element:

```
const canvas = document.getElementById('canvas');
const ctx = canvas.getContext('2d');
const width = canvas.width;
const height = canvas.height;
```

You'll need the **width** and **height** to randomly place each person onto the **canvas**, like this:

```
const people = Array(population)
  .fill()
  .map(() => {
    const x = Math.random() * width;
    const y = Math.random() * height;
    return new Person(x, y);
  });
```

Right now their positions are random. Unfortunately, patient 0 isn't. Time to give them some bad news:

```
people[0].infect();
```

With all this setup done you want to see where each person is:

```
const draw = () => {
  ctx.clearRect(0, 0, width, height);
  people.forEach((person) => {
    ctx.beginPath();
    ctx.arc(person.x, person.y, 5, 0, 2 * Math.PI);
    ctx.fillStyle = 'black';
    ctx.fill();
  });
};

draw();
```

When the **draw** function is run it will:

- clear the **canvas** (very important for animation)
- loop through each **person** in the **people** array
    o draw them as a dot on the **canvas**

Your **canvas** should look like this:

You made someone sick earlier, so they should be shown as a different colour:

```
ctx.fillStyle = 'black';
if (!person.alive) {
  ctx.fillStyle = 'lightgray';
} else if (person.infected) {
  ctx.fillStyle = 'red';
} else if (person.isImmune) {
  ctx.fillStyle = 'green';
}
```

By updating the code in the **draw** function you will be able to see four different states a **person** can go though: uninfected, deceased (not alive), infected and immune. Now the **canvas** should show patient zero as a red dot surrounded by 999 uninfected black dots.

You now need a way to update this simulation over time. It should be able to determine who will be infected based on their distance and infect them accordingly:

```
const update = () => {
  const uninfected = [];
  const infected = [];
```

Every time an **update** is made you need to perform a bunch of calculations based on each person's state – only living infected people can spread the infection, and those who are immune (or deceased) won't spread it:

```
people.forEach((person) => {
  if (person.alive && !person.isImmune) {
    if (person.infected) {
      infected.push(person);
    } else {
      uninfected.push(person);
    }
  }
  person.update();
});
```

This loop is also a great opportunity to call the **update** method of each person (every **update** is a new day). Now that you know who's infected and who isn't: time to write the logic that determines if someone's about to get sick.

```
infected.forEach((person) => {
  const contacts = uninfected.filter((otherPerson) => {
    const dx = Math.abs(person.x - otherPerson.x);
    const dy = Math.abs(person.y - otherPerson.y);
    const distance = Math.sqrt(Math.pow(dx, 2) + Math.pow(dy,
2));
    return distance < minDistance;
  });

  for (let i = 0; i < r0; i++) {
    const contact = contacts[Math.floor(Math.random() *
contacts.length)];
    if (contact) {
      contact.infect();
    }
  }
});
```

```
};
```

For each `infected` person you need to get the distance **between** them and every `uninfected` person. You already know the **x** and **y** position of each person, so to determine the distance you can use the Pythagorean theorem:

$$c^2 = a^2 + b^2$$

Or

$$distance = \sqrt{(x2 - x1)^2 + (y2 - y1)^2}$$

If this is new to you or you need a quick refresher, take a look at this diagram:

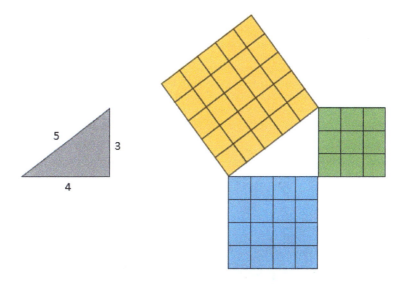

The area of the square made from the side length of 4 (*a*) plus the area of the square made from the side height of 3 (*b*) is the same as the area of the square made from the hypotenuse (the longest side of 5, *c*).

If an infected person is at 0,0 and an uninfected person is at 10,5:

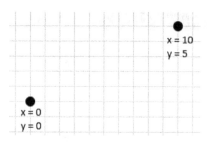

- $\sqrt{(10 - 0)^2 + (5 - 0)^2}$
- $\sqrt{10^2 + 5^2}$
- $\sqrt{100 + 25}$
- $\sqrt{125}$
- 11.18033

The **dx** and **dy** (difference of x, difference of y) are used in the area calculation and then the square root is used to give you the correct value. Using **Math.abs** tells JavaScript to ignore negative values: you don't know which of the two people you're trying to find the difference between is first or second.

Once you've filtered the potential **contacts** based on their distance you need to randomly choose which of the people will become infected based on the **r0** from earlier. Then you call the person's **infect** method and the class does the rest.

Let's say you want the simulation to run for 100 (simulated) days. Instead of using the **draw** function on its own you can use it with the **update** function inside a timer:

```
let count = 0;
const maxCount = 100;
const interval = setInterval(() => {
  update();
  draw();
  count++;
  if (count >= maxCount) {
    clearInterval(interval);
  }
}, 1000);   // <- use 100 if you want it faster
```

For the next 100 simulated days – with each of them being one regular second – the **update** function will run first to determine who's now infected and then the people will be drawn:

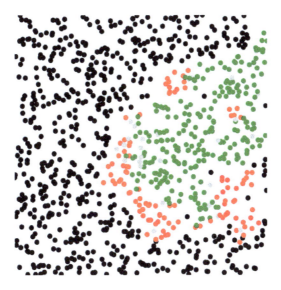

Your simulation will look different because the placement of the people will be random, but as long as the distance between infected and uninfected is less than the minimum distance then you'll be able to see how the disease spreads through the community.

The chance of survival for your simulated plague is 0.99, or 99%. Drop that to something lower:

```
const chanceSurvival = 0.75;
```

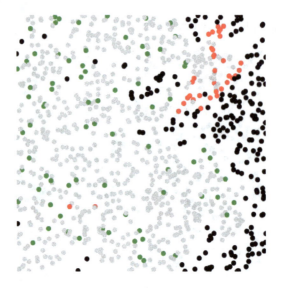

The reduced survival rate causes significantly fewer people surviving. This is because of the way the **r0** is used: every day it picks new people to infect, but this is supposed to represent the total number of people it will spread to during the infection. Some updates are needed.

You need to move the logic from the **update** method into your constructor:

```
this.isInfectious = false;
this.wontSurvive = Math.random() > chanceSurvival;
```

This is just for the simulation – in reality the chance of survival is not predetermined. The **wontSurvive** value replaces the random value:

```
if (this.health <= 0 || this.wontSurvive) {
    this.alive = false;
}
```

There's also the addition to the **infect** method:

```
infect() {
    this.isInfectious = true; // <- new
    this.infected = true;
}
```

And you need to add **isInfectious** to the **update** method:

```
if (this.daysInfected > 7) {
    this.isInfectious = false; ; // <- new
    this.infected = false;
    this.isImmune = true;
}
```

For this simulation once an infected person has passed it on, they shouldn't infect others. You just need to add a final change after the **r0** loop:

```
for (let i = 0; i < r0; i++) {
    // ...
}
person.isInfectious = false; // <- new
```

Now if you run your simulation with a 75% chance of survival it will show more realistic behaviour.

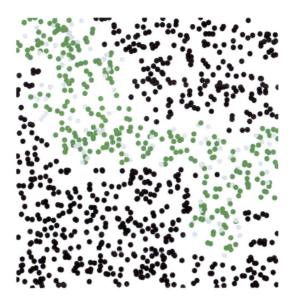

And if you want some more realism, the airborne measles virus has an **r0** of 12:

```
const r0 = 12;
const chanceSurvival = 0.998;
```

You can look up the `r0` and survival rates of other infectious diseases and see what happens with them. Change the minimum distance and the population to see how it changes the results. Your simulation could stop due to the distance between people being too far for it to spread, or you might see the infection in half the population before it swings around and goes for the other half.

There are more changes you can make: you could update it so those with an existing immunity would have a reduced chance of infecting others, or those who are infected self-isolate (increase their distance from others) to stop the spread.

Image filters

You've been asked to create some filter effects for user avatars. The user should be able to choose an image and have an effect applied to it before it's saved. The effects will be:

- convert to grayscale
- add static
- convert to sepia
- blur

To start, you'll need some HTML:

```
<!DOCTYPE html>
<html lang="en">
  <head>
    <meta charset="UTF-8" />
    <title>Filters</title>
  </head>
  <body>
    <input type="file" id="fileInput" accept="image/*" />

    <img id="image" src="" alt="Image" />
    <canvas id="canvas"></canvas>

    <script src="./image-filters.js"></script>
```

```
  </body>
</html>
```

The **input** element will enable users to choose an image. Do you see the **accept** attribute? Right now it allows for all images but you might want to change that later. There's also the **image** and **canvas** elements. The **image** will be used to show what the user will select while the **canvas** will show the image plus the effect.

```
const fileInput = document.getElementById('fileInput');
const image = document.getElementById('image');
const canvas = document.getElementById('canvas');
const output = canvas.getContext('2d');
```

These variables will enable you to reference the elements in the HTML page. A user can click the button right now and choose a file, but it won't do anything else. JavaScript needs to listen for a change:

```
fileInput.addEventListener('change', (e) => {
  const file = e.target.files[0];
  const url = URL.createObjectURL(file);

  image.src = url;

  URL.revokeObjectURL(url);
});
```

When a change occurs the listener supplies an event (**e**) that contains a reference to the file. To show it in an **image**, you convert the file into a URL and update the image's **src** attribute. To prevent memory leaks, you need to revoke the URL when it's no longer needed.

Time to give it a test: press the 'Browse' button and choose an image:

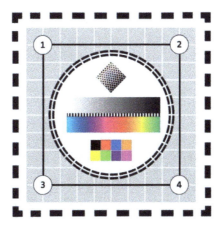

You can use any JPEG, GIF or PNG image – just make sure the resolution is small (width and height of around 500 pixels) to help you with testing.

To add effects to the image you need to get it into the **canvas**, but only after the image has finished loading into the browser. Another event listener is needed:

```
image.addEventListener('load', () => {
  canvas.width = image.width;
  canvas.height = image.height;
  output.drawImage(image, 0, 0);
});
```

Once the **image** element has finished loading the URL you can draw it right into the **canvas**. You now have the ability to access the data and make changes with your filters. This is what the majority of each filter will look like:

```
const filter = (ctx, width, height) => {
  const { data } = ctx.getImageData(0, 0, width, height);

  // ... apply filter ...

  const imageData = new ImageData(data, width, height);
  ctx.putImageData(imageData, 0, 0);
};
```

Whenever a filter is run it needs to get the most up-to-date version of the image data from the `canvas`. Why? If you decide to add multiple filters then you'd want to layer them over the top of each other. If you keep the original image data in a variable and use then then you could only use one image filter as it would override any changes.

The first filter is to convert the `canvas` to grayscale:

```
const convertToGrayscale = (ctx, width, height) => {
  const { data } = ctx.getImageData(0, 0, width, height);
  const grayscaleData = new Uint8ClampedArray(data.length);

  for (let i = 0; i < data.length; i += 4) {
    const [r, g, b] = data.slice(i, i + 3);
    const average = (r + g + b) / 3;
    grayscaleData[i] = average;
    grayscaleData[i + 1] = average;
    grayscaleData[i + 2] = average;
    grayscaleData[i + 3] = 255;
  }

  const grayscaleImageData =
    new ImageData(grayscaleData, width, height);
  ctx.putImageData(grayscaleImageData, 0, 0);
};
```

Each pixel in the data is represented by three values, or channels: red, green, blue and alpha (or transparency). Converting them to grayscale is achieved by taking the red (r), green (g) and blue (b) colour channels of the current pixel, averaging them and then using that value for the all of them.

If you have a pixel that's completely red:

Pixel = 255 0 0
Average = (255 + 0 + 0) / 3 = 85

It would be the same if the pixel was completely green or blue. Grayscale is just a difference between the brightness of the pixels (actual colours are gone). The `grayscaleData` uses `Uint8ClampedArray`, and that includes an extra channel: alpha (or transparency). You can set that to **255**.

You can now add that filter to the loader (along with the **output**, `canvas width` and `height`):

```
image.addEventListener('load', () => {
  canvas.width = image.width;
  canvas.height = image.height;
  output.drawImage(image, 0, 0);

  convertToGrayscale(output, canvas.width, canvas.height);
  // ...
```

If you select an image now you should see a side-by-side view of the original image and its grayscale version:

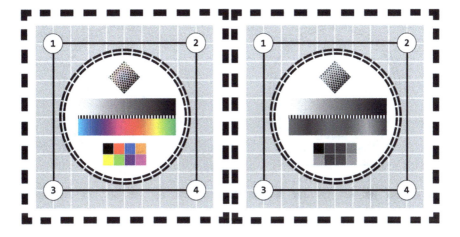

Next is the addStatic filter:

```
const addStatic = (ctx, width, height, amount) => {
  const { data } = ctx.getImageData(0, 0, width, height);
  for (let i = 0; i < data.length; i += 4) {
    if (Math.random() < amount) {
      data[i] = Math.random() * 255;
      data[i + 1] = Math.random() * 255;
      data[i + 2] = Math.random() * 255;
    }
  }
  const staticImageData = new ImageData(data, width, height);
  ctx.putImageData(staticImageData, 0, 0);
};
```

In this case static is corrupted data, so when you're looping through the pixel data you can change some of them to be completely different values. Just comment-out the call to the grayscale filter and add the new one:

```
// convertToGrayscale(output, canvas.width, canvas.height);
addStatic(output, canvas.width, canvas.height, 0.2);
```

You can change the **amount** argument to other values, but **0.2** looks like this:

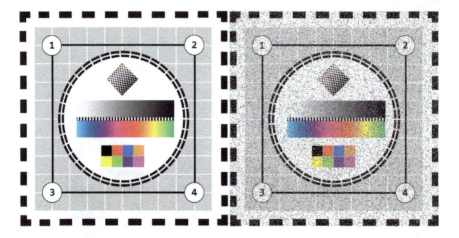

Converting the image to sepia is similar to grayscale:

```
const convertToSepia = (ctx, width, height) => {
  const { data } = ctx.getImageData(0, 0, width, height);

  for (let i = 0; i < data.length; i += 4) {
    const [r, g, b] = data.slice(i, i + 3);

    const newR = r * 0.393 + g * 0.769 + b * 0.189;
    const newG = r * 0.349 + g * 0.686 + b * 0.168;
    const newB = r * 0.272 + g * 0.534 + b * 0.131;

    data[i] = newR;
    data[i + 1] = newG;
    data[i + 2] = newB;
```

```
    }

    const sepiaImageData = new ImageData(data, width, height);
    ctx.putImageData(sepiaImageData, 0, 0);
};
```

Instead of averaging the channels together you're changing them. Those hard-coded values are the same as other sepia filters to emulate the look of old sepia photographs which appear warmer than the grayscale version. You can add the function call with the others:

```
// convertToGrayscale(output, canvas.width, canvas.height);
// addStatic(output, canvas.width, canvas.height, 0.2);
convertToSepia(output, canvas.width, canvas.height);
```

Here's what the sepia version looks like:

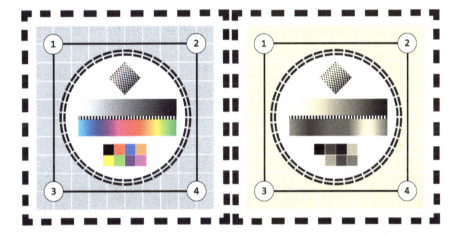

The last filter is the gaussian blur. This is very different from the others as it transforms a pixel based on the pixels surrounding it:

```
const gaussianBlur = (ctx, width, height, blurRadius) => {
  const { data } = ctx.getImageData(0, 0, width, height);
  const blurredData = new Uint8ClampedArray(data.length);

  for (let y = 0; y < height; y++) {
    for (let x = 0; x < width; x++) {
```

The other filters have all looped though the **data**, but because you need to know what the neighbouring pixels are it's easier to use the **height** and **width**.

```
let sumRed = 0;
let sumGreen = 0;
let sumBlue = 0;
let count = 0;

for (let ky = -blurRadius; ky <= blurRadius; ky++) {
  for (let kx = -blurRadius; kx <= blurRadius; kx++) {
```

The blur works by looping through the neighbouring pixels and totalling up the values of each red, green and blue channel:

-1,-1	0,-1	1,-1
-1,0	0,0	1,0
-1,1	0,1	1,1

```
let nx = x + kx;
let ny = y + ky;

if (nx >= 0 && nx < canvas.width &&
    ny >= 0 && ny < canvas.height) {
```

Quick check to make sure the pixel you're about to use is actually on the **canvas**. Now you can start adding the channel data.

```
let index = (ny * canvas.width + nx) * 4;
sumRed += data[index];
sumGreen += data[index + 1];
sumBlue += data[index + 2];
```

```
                count++;
            }
        }
    }
```

Once the sum for each channel is ready it's then averaged:

```
    const index = (y * canvas.width + x) * 4;
    blurredData[index] = sumRed / count;
    blurredData[index + 1] = sumGreen / count;
    blurredData[index + 2] = sumBlue / count;
    blurredData[index + 3] = data[index + 3];
    }
  }
  const blurredImageData = new ImageData(blurredData, width,
height);
  ctx.putImageData(blurredImageData, 0, 0);
};
```

The result is the colours of the neighbouring pixels are merged into the current one, and this causes the blur effect.

Like the others you can add the call to the loader:

```
// convertToGrayscale(output, canvas.width, canvas.height);
// addStatic(output, canvas.width, canvas.height, 0.2);
// convertToSepia(output, canvas.width, canvas.height);
gaussianBlur(output, canvas.width, canvas.height, 2);
```

And don't forget the **blurRadius** argument. The larger that number is the more time it will take as there's more pixels it needs to process. And here's the result:

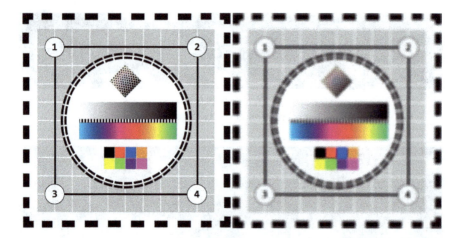

There are other filters you can create. You could:

- reduce the number of colours
    - divide the channel's value by the number of colours, round it, then multiply the value by the same number of colours)
- swap the channels
    - create a new variable to store one of the channels as you reassign them
- shift the colours to make them cooler (or warmer)
    - add or subtract the amount or red or blue in each pixel
- flip or rotate the image
    - when looping through the width (horizontal flip) or height (vertical flip) use the value of the pixel that's at the opposite end of the array

Entirely up to you! Enjoy.

Sums of random distribution

Disclaimer: This project contains elements of gambling. If you have an issue with gambling or addictive personality traits that could be triggered then this project is *not for you*. Gambling addiction destroys lives and neither the author or publisher will not be held liable for your actions. Please seek help if this relates to you and <u>do not progress further</u>. If you like maths, are someone who likes numbers, or an engineer who likes to see order come from chaos, then please continue.

A relative of yours has found out that you're 'good with numbers' and wants to know why some numbers in a dice game occur more frequently than others. For a single die:

```
const faces = [1, 2, 3, 4, 5, 6];
const roleDie = () => Math.ceil(Math.random() * faces.length);

for (let i = 0; i < 10; i++) {
  console.log(roleDie());
}
```

You can roll the die as many times as you want and receive a random number in return. In fact, you can roll it 1,000 times to see what values you get:

```
const distribution = faces.reduce((acc, face) => {
  acc[`Side ${face}`] = 0;
  return acc;
}, {});

for (let i = 0; i < 1000; i++) {
  const face = roleDie();
  distribution[`Side ${face}`]++;
}
```

The **distribution**, or the number of times each die was rolled, may look similar to this:

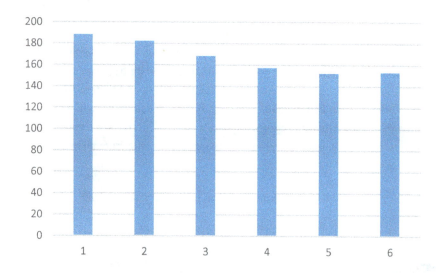

Your **distribution** will be different, but overall the numbers will be unremarkable. Don't let the Gambler's Fallacy fool you, dice don't have a memory so you should have no 'expectation' of a particular value: in this example the numbers 4, 5 and 6 are not *expected*, *next* or *overdue*.

Many games use more than one die. Often the sum of the two dice is the core of the game, and some of these sums appear to have a greater chance of being rolled:

```
const values = {};
for (let i = 0; i < 10000; i++) {
  const face1 = roleDie();
```

```
  const face2 = roleDie();
  const value = face1 + face2;
  values[value] = (values[value] || 0) + 1;
}
console.log(values);
```

Which makes a lot of sense: there are more combinations that can be added together between two dice that equal 7 (1 + 6, 2 + 5, 3 + 4) than the combinations that equal 2 (just 1 + 1). The distribution of that looks like this:

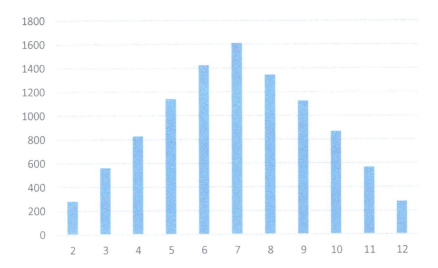

Your chances of rolling a sum of 6, 7 or 8 using two dice are much higher than rolling a 2 or 12. Despite each individual die giving a random value the sum is *not as random*. With enough dice rolls a sum of 7 will be more frequent.

Your relative is happy with your answer. But you're not: what could be done to prove this hypothesis in other games?

Some games don't use dice – they use balls. Large ones with numbers painted on them. And if you correctly guess which numbers are drawn then you could win a prize. To begin:

```
const ballCount = 45;
const balls = Array(ballCount)
  .fill()
  .map((_, i) => i + 1);
```

This creates an array with 45 balls (fake ones, not real ones). For each game that's played you need to randomly pick some of them.

```javascript
const draw = (balls, drawn) => {
  const freshBalls = [...balls];
  const result = [];
  for (let i = 0; i < drawn; i++) {
    const index = Math.floor(Math.random() * freshBalls.length);
    result.push(freshBalls.splice(index, 1)[0]);
  }
  return result;
};

console.log(draw(balls, 6));
```

When the **draw** function is called it makes a copy of the **balls** array. The loop will choose a ball at random and **push** it into the **result** array. It will also remove that ball from the list so it can't be picked again. Your output should be something like this:

```
[ 18, 26, 11, 22, 20, 44 ]
```

Great! Now you need to simulate multiple games:

```javascript
const ballsToDraw = 6;
const simulations = 1000;
const games = {};
Array(simulations)
  .fill()
  .map(() => {
    const game = draw(balls, ballsToDraw);
    const sum = game.reduce((acc, ball) => acc + ball, 0);
    games[sum] = (games[sum] || 0) + 1;
  });
```

Just like the dice version: it creates a new **game** with the **draw** function and adds the values together. It then uses the **sum** as an object key and increments the value by 1.

This allows you to get a distribution of sums to determine if any have a greater chance of appearing.

```
console.log(games);
```

The exact values will vary, but towards the middle of the output you should see that a few of the **sum** values are larger than others. This makes sense because of the greater number of combinations that would equal the sum. If the minimum and maximum sum of the two dice are 2 and 12, the minimum and maximum sum of the ball combinations would be:

- $1 + 2 + 3 + 4 + 5 + 6 = 21$
- $40 + 41 + 42 + 43 + 44 + 45 = 255$

Those are the only combinations that will equal 21 and 255. But how many combinations would equal 125?

As far as your original hypothesis is concerned: you're correct. Despite the balls being randomly drawn the **sum** has some not-so-random behaviour. Can this be taken further? If you know which sums are more likely to 'win' based on the previous history, is it be possible to determine which combination of balls would produce the same sums?

Let's check out the top five:

```
const maxCount = 5;
const topGames = Object.entries(games)
  .map(([sum, count]) => ({ sum, count }))
  .sort((a, b) => b.count - a.count)
  .slice(0, maxCount);

console.log(topGames);
```

And now get the **sums**:

```
const sums = topGames.map((game) => parseInt(game.sum));
console.log(sums);
```

You should see something like this:

```
[ { sum: '139', count: 20 },
  { sum: '147', count: 20 },
```

```
    { sum: '112', count: 17 },
    { sum: '130', count: 17 },
    { sum: '134', count: 17 } ]
```

Keep in mind this is the top five across 1,000 simulated games. It's not a guaranteed win, but for this project the **sums** are the goal: any combination of balls that produce the same sum could be viable options.

```
const combinations = sums.map((sum) => {
  const freshBalls = [...balls];
  const results = [];
  while (results.length < 5) {
    const game = draw(freshBalls, ballsToDraw);
    const gameSum = game.reduce((acc, ball) => acc + ball, 0);
    if (gameSum === sum) {
      results.push(game);
    }
  }

  return {
    sum,
    results
  };
});
```

This is another brute-force approach. Just like before when drawing a new game a fresh set of balls are used. For each **sum** you want five new combinations (or any number) where the game's sum is the same. Check it out:

```
console.log(JSON.stringify(combinations, null, 2));
```

Adding the numbers of each combination together should equal the sum (the object's key). These simulated games are also random, but are they viable? To check if these games could have been winners you need to store a record of the simulated games. Go back to where you're simulating the games and add a **playedGames** array:

```
const ballsToDraw = 6;
const simulations = 1000;
const games = {};
const playedGames = []; // <- new
Array(simulations)
  .fill()
  .map(() => {
    const game = draw(balls, ballsToDraw);
    const sum = game.reduce((acc, ball) => acc + ball, 0);
    games[sum] = (games[sum] || 0) + 1;
    playedGames.push(game); // <- new
  });
```

This new array will have all the games that were played. Now to check if any of the simulated ones could have been winners:

```
const simulatedGames = combinations.map((combo) =>
  combo.results
).flat();
```

The original combinations used key/value pairs, but you only need the values.

```
const minMatches = 3;
const matches = simulatedGames.filter((simGame) => {
  const filtered = playedGames.filter((game) => {
    const count = game.filter((ball) =>
      simGame.includes(ball)).length;
    return count >= minMatches;
  });

  return filtered.length;
});

console.log(`${simulatedGames.length} simulated games created`);
console.log(`${matches.length} simulated games share
${minMatches} balls`);
console.log(matches.map((game) => game.join(', ')));
```

The `minMatches` determines how many balls in each of the `simulatedGames` need to match the real ones to be returned. Your output will differ, but you should get the number of simulated games it created, the number that could have won and the games themselves:

```
25 simulated games created
5 simulated games share 3 balls
[ '38, 45, 23, 14, 40, 28',
  '10, 29, 43, 33, 37, 36',
  '3, 9, 18, 38, 5, 1',
  '11, 40, 2, 36, 22, 10',
  '7, 18, 23, 1, 28, 44' ]
```

You can get different results by changing the `maxCount` for the `topGames`, the number of `combinations` within the `while` loop (currently 5) and the `minMatches` (currently 3).

Remember that the `simulatedGames` uses historical data that was generated with `Math.random()` in your browser. It does not represent a truly random value as software and machines can only fake random numbers. It's likely that you'll get different results if you attempt to use this with real-world data: that's going to be genuinely random.

Also: the `simulatedGames` only exists because of the previous numbers. Just because you get a match doesn't mean it will win in the future: it would have won in the past. Treat this as nothing more than an experiment in random numbers and leave it at that.

Conclusion

You've made it to the end. Well done! You should be proud with all the work you've completed to get here. From the basics of variables, conditions, loops and functions you've been able to write the core mechanics of various games, dabbled in cryptocurrency's proof-of-work system, simulated a variety of scenarios and created machine learning models to predict and classify data.

Some of the projects you've worked on – like the charts, drawing and machine learning – can be taken further using third-party libraries. The foundations you created have given you a practical understanding these concepts, giving you an edge over other engineers. You'll also greatly appreciate that work others have done to simplify the technology. You're also more likely to have fewer issues than other engineers because of your earlier effort and the experience you've had.

And like all things there's so much more to learn. New API features are being released all the time and new demands on technology mean that you'll always need to keep your skills up-to-date. So keep coding and enjoy your new journey as a JavaScript engineer!

Reserved words

abstract	double	in	super
arguments	else	instanceof	switch
await	enum	int	synchronized
boolean	eval	interface	this
break	export	let	throw
byte	extends	long	throws
case	false/FALSE	native	transient
catch	final	new	true/TRUE
char	finally	null	try
class	float	package	typeof
const	for	private	var
continue	function	protected	void
debugger	goto	public	volatile
default	if	return	while
delete	implements	short	with
do	import	static	yield

References

Airbnb. (2016). *Enzyme* [Web technology]. https://airbnb.io/projects/enzyme/

Apple Inc. (2003, January 7). *Safari* [Software]. https://apps.apple.com/no/app/safari/id1146562112

Buursma, B., & Hoone, I. V. (2017). *CodeSandbox* [Web]. https://codesandbox.io/

Coyer, C., Sabat, T., & Vazquez, A. (2012). *CodePen* [Web]. https://codepen.io/

Dahl, R., & OpenJS Foundation. (2009, May 27). *Node.js* [Software]. https://nodejs.org/en

Eich, B., Netscape, & community. (1995, December 4). *JavaScript* [Web technology]. Netscape.

Mozilla. (2004, November 9). *Firefox* [Software]. https://www.mozilla.org/en-US/firefox/

Gardner, J. (2013, March 27). *Tell, Show, Do, Apply: The Anatomy Of Good Instruction*. eLearning Industry. https://elearningindustry.com/tell-show-do-apply-the-anatomy-of-good-instruction

Google. (2008). *Google Chrome* [Software]. https://www.google.com/intl/en_au/chrome/dr/download

Hash Functions. (n.d.). York University. http://www.cse.yorku.ca/~oz/hash.html

Harris, R., Faubert, A., Hau, T. L., McCann, B., Holthausen, S., & contributors. (2016, November 26). *Svelte* [Web technology]. https://svelte.dev/

Hatos, S., Clark, D., Greenberg, R., Hall, M., Hall, S., Garfinkle, D., Renfoe, J., Mirkin, J., Richards, M., & Quinn, J. (Executive Producers). (1963 – present). *Let's Make a Deal* [TV series]. NBC/ABC; CBS.

IEEE 754. (2024, April 20). In *Wikipedia*. https://en.wikipedia.org/wiki/IEEE_754

Jammot, A. (1965). *Des chiffres et des lettres*. [Television show].

Kernighan, B. W., & Ritchie, D. M. (1988). *The C programming Language*. https://www.cimat.mx/ciencia_para_jovenes/bachillerato/libros/%5BKernigh an-Ritchie%5DThe_C_Programming_Language.pdf

Krawczyk, O., & Zalewa, P. (2010). *JSFiddle* [Web]. https://jsfiddle.net/

Mann, B. (2014). *Cypress* [Web technology]. https://cypress.io

Microsoft. (2015). *Microsoft Edge* [Software]. https://www.microsoft.com/en-us/edge

Microsoft. (2015, April 29). *Visual Studio Code* [Software]. https://code.visualstudio.com/

Massachusetts Institute of Technology. (n.d.). *The MIT License*. https://opensource.org/licenses/MIT

Munroe, R. (n.d.). *Password Strength* [Comic]. https://xkcd.com/936/

Netscape. (1995, December 4). *Netscape and Sun Announce JavaScript, the Open, Cross-Platform Object Scripting Language for Enterprise Networks and the Internet*. Netscape Communications. https://web.archive.org/web/20070916144913/https://wp.netscape.com/new sref/pr/newsrelease67.html

OpenJS Foundation. (n.d.). *Jest* [Web technology]. https://jestjs.io

OpenJS Foundation. (2011, November 22). *Mocha* [Web technology]. https://mochajs.org

Oracle. (n.d.) *Applets* [Web technology]. https://www.oracle.com/java/technologies/applets.html

Sharp, R. (n.d.). *JS Bin* [Web]. https://jsbin.com/

Valenzuela, A. (2023, November 21). *Gambler's Fallacy | Definition, Psychology & Examples*. Study.com. https://study.com/learn/lesson/gamblers-fallacy-overview-examples.html

Walke, J., & Meta. (2013, May 29). *React* [Web technology]. https://react.dev/

Wardle, J. (2021, October). *Wordle* [Web]. New York Times. https://www.nytimes.com/games/wordle/index.html

Whittle, R. (1999, October 18). *DSP generation of Pink (1/f) Noise*. https://www.firstpr.com.au/dsp/pink-noise/

You, E. (2014). *Vue* [Web technology]. https://vuejs.org/

Index

www.ingramcontent.com/pod-product-compliance
Lightning Source LLC
Chambersburg PA
CBHW071104050326
40690CB00008B/1104